THE GLORIOUS YEARS OF THE GWR

GREAT WESTERN RAILWAY

PETER TUFFREY

GREAT NORTHERN

ACKNOWLEDGEMENTS

I would like to thank the following people for their help: Roger Arnold, David Burrill, John Chalcraft, Paul Chancellor, Peter Crangle, John Law, Hugh Parkin, Bill Reed, David P. Williams.

Special thanks are due to my son Tristram Tuffrey for his help and encouragement throughout the course of the project.

Unless otherwise stated, all photographs from the author's collection.

In the latter years of the GWR, colour photography had only just begun and was an expensive activity that very few photographers could afford. Consequently less than 50 colour photographs of GWR subjects are known to have survived, and the quality of these in many cases is poor. The author would like to express sincere thanks to David P. Williams for his skill in producing the fine colour illustrations on the front and back covers of this book. They have been painstakingly put together by digitally adding colour to original monochrome photographs, with the aim of recreating what the photographer could see in the camera viewfinder when the shutter was released.

Front cover: GWR No 6008 'King James II' is seen at Paddington preparing to leave with an express. Entering service in March 1928, No 6008 was initially based at Plymouth Laira for two years and then spent 22 years from August 1930 at Wolverhampton Stafford Rd before returning to Laira in June 1952. It finally ended its days back at Stafford Rd from February 1959 to June 1962. In this 1928 photograph the locomotive is seen in original condition. The upper lamp bracket sits at the top of the smokebox with its accompanying footstep in place on the smokebox door, whilst the original smoothed and rounded style of casing over the inside valve chest is clear to see, as is the original design of outside steam pipes.

Back cover colour picture: GWR King Class 4-6-0 No 6000 'King George V' is seen at Southcote near Reading with the Cornish Riviera Express in the 1930s. It carries the bell presented in 1927 on the occasion of No 6000's visit to Baltimore to celebrate the centenary of America's oldest railroad.

Great Northern Books Limited
PO Box 1380, Bradford, BD5 5FB
www.greatnorthernbooks.co.uk

© Peter Tuffrey 2024

Every effort has been made to acknowledge correctly and contact the copyright holders of material in this book. Great Northern Books Ltd apologises for any unintentional errors or omissions, which should be notified to the publisher.

All rights reserved. No part of this book may be reproduced in any form or by any means without permission in writing from the publisher, except by a reviewer who may quote brief passages in a review.

ISBN: 978-1-914227-74-5

Design and layout: David Burrill

CIP Data
A catalogue for this book is available from the British Library

INTRODUCTION

The Great Western Railway started as the result of local businessmen in Bristol being inspired by the success of the first railway undertakings and the quick realisation that other places with better connections could oust the city as a primary shipping point. They resolved to build a better line than hitherto imagined and the GWR was born in January 1833, with Isambard Kingdom Brunel soon appointed as the company's engineer. He took the bold step of choosing a different gauge than that in use at the time. Originally, 7 ft, later 7 ft 0¼ in. and known as Broad Gauge, Brunel favoured this because greater stability at higher speeds was achieved in comparison to 4 ft 8½ in. or Standard Gauge used by other companies.

From receiving the authorising Act of Parliament in 1835, three years elapsed before the first section was ready from a temporary terminus near the later site of Paddington station to Taplow. The remaining 130 miles gradually came into use for the complete opening during June 1841.

Even when the main line was under construction, the GWR was active in making other connections. In 1839, the company entered an arrangement to work the Bristol & Exeter Railway which opened the first section in mid-June 1841 and was ready throughout during 1844. Around this time, the GWR prepared to acquire the Cheltenham & Great Western Union Railway. The company started a project to join the main line at Swindon and reach Gloucester and Cheltenham. Only managing to lay a line to Cirencester, the GWR stepped in to finish the project.

As the 1850s began, the GWR began operating services on the South Wales Railway which Brunel engineered to the Broad Gauge. The first section was between Chepstow and Swansea. A connection was made with the GWR at Gloucester in 1851 and a bridge over the River Wye at Chepstow was necessary, not being ready until 1852. Four years later, the route stretched across to Neyland. The GWR leased the SWR for around ten years before amalgamation was carried out.

Whilst the company spread westward, a connection to the north was deemed necessary. As the branch to Oxford had been built, the extension of this to Rugby was authorised allowing a junction with the London & Birmingham Railway. In the event this project only reached Banbury and a new company was formed to divert westward to Leamington and Birmingham. This section was ready during 1852. In a strategic move, the GWR had absorbed the Birmingham, Wolverhampton & Dudley Railway in 1847 and connected with this in the early 1850s. The route used some of the Oxford, Worcester & Wolverhampton Railway to reach Wolverhampton. Soon after, the GWR acquired the Shrewsbury & Birmingham and Shrewsbury & Chester Railways.

The S&BR and S&CR saw the GWR gain possession of Standard Gauge lines and rolling stock. From the early 1840s, the Birmingham & Gloucester Railway highlighted a problem of the growing, competing network of railways. The connection with the Bristol & Gloucester Railway was initially impractical owing to the different gauges. In the mid-1840s a Royal Commission was established to report on the issue and found in favour of Standard Gauge, though railways in the South West and those connecting with the GWR could still be built to the Broad Gauge. Mixed Gauges were also used in certain locations. By 1861, Broad Gauge was out of favour as Standard Gauge lines were installed in Paddington station and at the end of the decade the first conversions were carried out on the Oxford to Wolverhampton line, in addition to the short section from Reading to Basingstoke. A major step towards Standard Gauge was the South Wales Railway changeover in 1872, as well as the connection from Swindon to Gloucester. The Broad Gauge was finally abolished over the weekend of 21-22 May 1892.

By this time the GWR's territory had expanded considerably. In the mid-1870s the company formally took over the South Devon Railway and West Cornwall Railway running from Exeter to Plymouth and Truro to Penzance respectively. The section between Plymouth and Truro was leased to the GWR until the late 1880s when also absorbed.

Along with the SWR, the Vale of Neath Railway, Pontypool, Caerleon & Newport Railway, Monmouthshire Railway & Canal Company, Carmarthen & Cardigan Railway, Manchester & Milford Railway, etc., gave the GWR a presence in Wales. Although the GWR was relatively unchallenged in the South West, the company operated against several rivals in Wales. Companies promoted to connect Central Wales ultimately came together to form the Cambrian Railways and industrial South Wales had a group of independent operations to maximise steel and coal profits – Taff Vale Railway, Barry Railway, Rhymney Railway, etc. The London & North Western Railway also challenged in the country by crossing from Shrewsbury to Swansea through taking over small companies. In the North, the LNWR monopolised the route to Ireland between Chester & Holyhead.

Following many amalgamations in the 1880s and 1890s, the GWR had just a dozen in the years before the First World War. This left the company free to develop the network, improve services and rolling stock. Several new lines were built to eliminate some of the mistakes created in the construction of the system by original companies, as well as for better connections. An example of the latter being a new line from Wooton Bassett to the Severn Tunnel which removed the need to travel via Bristol. Also, a shorter route from High Wycombe to London was created in a joint venture with the Great Central Railway. George Jackson Churchward became Chief Mechanical Engineer in 1902 following a spell as William Dean's assistant making him well-placed to revamp the GWR's rolling stock to modern standards. The result of this was an improvement in services, like the introduction of a Paddington to Plymouth express which ran non-stop over the 245.7 miles – a world record at the time. Coaching stock was upgraded allowing a rise in the standard offered by the GWR.

At the outbreak of the First World War, the railways in Britain were placed under Government control for the duration of the conflict. The GWR was affected through the loss of men to the Armed Forces and a change in focus to assisting the war effort. At Swindon Works priorities shifted to munitions work, such as high explosive shells, guns, gun carriages, and construction of road wagons, as well as ambulance trains. Locomotives were also requisitioned and shipped overseas.

When the conflict was over, a select committee gathered data to make recommendations for the future. Sir Eric Geddes of the North Eastern Railway led the task and in 1920 he presented a white paper suggesting regional groups of railways. He was against Nationalisation as being an unwieldy enterprise with lack of accountability and likely source of financial waste.

In the passage of the Railways Act 1921 the idea of splitting into regions was modified to larger areas organised along operating the main lines. As the GWR had the most route miles in the South West and in Wales, the company became the dominant force in the ensuing amalgamations for Grouping and was unique amongst other companies across Britain in retaining the original company title. Along with several previously mentioned competing companies, over two dozen smaller companies fell under the GWR's authority from 1st January 1923. At this time the GWR had over 3,000 route miles, nearly 4,000 locomotives, approx. 6,400 carriages, just less than 100,000 wagons and 110,000 employees.

The GWR was much bigger than the constituent railways and had much more consistency from 1923. The company continued to offer premier passenger services, such as the ocean liner trains, named services like the 'Cornish Riviera Express', 'Torbay Limited', 'Cheltenham Spa Express', etc. In the late 1920s, the GWR experimented with a Pullman carriage service, though high charges saw a switch to Swindon-built carriages, the super saloons. As new motive power was provided in the 1920s, the speed of expresses was improved on a number of trains. The decade also saw motor vehicle use by the GWR rise as road transport gained popularity for cost and ease of movement. The GWR subsequently invested in a number of existing road companies rather than start fresh businesses. A new service introduced by the GWR in 1928 was Land Cruises where excursions were offered in open-top buses on scenic routes in the company's territory.

As a result of the financial crisis of 1929, many businesses faced a difficult entry into the 1930s, including the GWR and the other railway companies. Despite these challenges, new and improved rolling stock was built at Swindon, including Grange Class 4-6-0s, 2884 Class 2-8-0s and 8750 Class 0-6-0PT locomotives. Also, streamlined diesel railcars were built for local trains following on from the GWR's introduction of several dozen steam rail motors in the early 20th century. For an experiment, the GWR built some articulated carriages for express services, whilst the 'Cornish Riviera Express' had new coaches for the 1935 season. To cater for group travel, the company introduced open carriages called the excursion stock and for holidaymakers redundant coaches were repurposed as accommodation at places of natural beauty across the system. Thanks to Government assistance introduced to keep employment high in the Depression, new works were undertaken, including new marshalling yards, lines, goods depots, engine and carriage sheds, signalling and workshop improvements.

As had been the case in the 1914-1918 conflict, the railway companies were taken under Government control for the duration of the Second World War. The GWR contributed to the war effort in areas including: preparation for the conflict; locomotive construction (some to Stanier's 8F Class design); specialised carriage production (ambulance trains); and munitions work, such as anti-aircraft guns, bombs, etc. For D-Day, the company handled 24,000 special trains and moved 230,000 members of the armed services. In the month after the invasion, a further 17,500 linked services ran on the GWR. Ten thousand new staff members were recruited during the war, many of which were women who numbered 16,000 employees in 1945.

With the war over, the political mood of the country favoured the Labour movement. The party claimed power in 1945 on the basis of establishing a Welfare State, providing a National Health Service and Nationalising many British industries. Amongst the latter were the railway companies which had suffered during the war and faced a difficult rebuilding process. The Transport Act 1947 created the British Transport Commission to oversee the new British Railways, along with road haulage, canals, ports, buses. Much of the GWR became British Railways Western Region, ending over 100 years of the company's continuous operation.

Although the GWR ceased to exist, the traditions of the company persisted with the staff and enthusiasts into the new era. This was to last with steam for just over a decade as the Modernisation Plan called for the traction's elimination, whilst the Beeching Report culled stations from the network. A number of withdrawn steam locomotives were sold for scrap to Woodham Brothers, Barry, South Wales, and the company allowed stock to accumulate. This left many ex-GWR locomotives to be saved and restored, with around 140 surviving to the present. Similarly, enthusiasts were dismayed at the closure of many lines and projects to restore the railways as heritage sites emerged. In South West England there are several preserved routes: Bodmin & Wenford; West Somerset; Swanage; Helston; Somerset & Dorset Railway Heritage Trust; Tarka Valley line. The Didcot Railway Centre and STEAM Museum, Swindon, are also dedicated to the history of the GWR. Recently, the private train operating company serving the South West and South Wales has rebranded as Great Western Railway meaning the original company is still revered, fondly remembered and celebrated as we approach 200 years from the creation of 'God's Wonderful Railway' in 1833.

Peter Tuffrey
Doncaster, May 2024

BROAD GAUGE LOCOMOTIVES

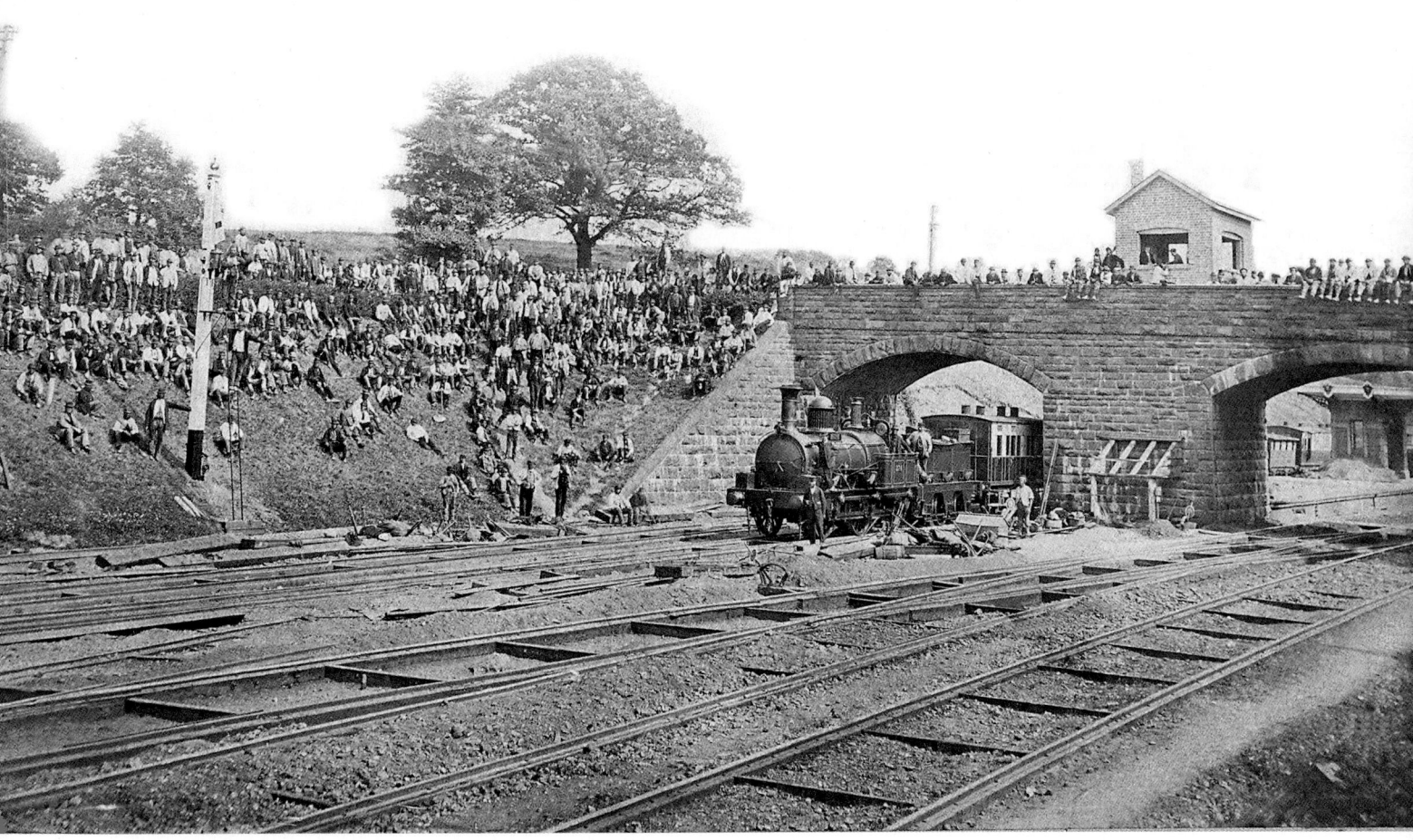

Above **GRANGE COURT STATION – NO. 274**

Early railways used different gauges, though the more successful ones, such as the Liverpool & Manchester Railway and Stockton & Darlington Railway, favoured 4 ft 8 in., which was later expanded to 4 ft 8½ in. As these companies grew and new ones formed, 4 ft 8½ in. or Standard Gauge was widely in use. Yet, Isambard Kingdom Brunel, engineer for the Great Western Railway, decided a gauge of 7 ft, later 7 ft 0¼ in. known as Broad Gauge, was desirable to provide greater stability for the rolling stock. The company and associated railways continued with Broad Gauge even when a Royal Commission reported on the matter and an Act favouring Standard Gauge was passed. In time, Standard Gauge proliferated leaving the GWR obliged to cater for railways that connected with the Broad Gauge. This was not convenient and by the late 1860s parts of the system began to be converted. The line between Oxford and Wolverhampton, as well as that from Reading to Basingstoke switched to Standard Gauge in April 1869, then in late summer Grange Court to Hereford made the changeover. The process continued gradually until the last Broad Gauge service operated on 20th May 1892. This image was captured some time before the end at Grange Court station in 1869 as the conversion was being carried out. The facility had been opened by the Hereford, Ross & Gloucester Railway during June 1855 and was briefly part of the West Midland Railway before amalgamation with the GWR in 1863. The locomotive present is no. 274 which was built for the Newport, Abergavenny & Hereford Railway in the late 1850s by E.B. Wilson & Co., Hunslet, and later became part of WMR stock. No. 274 went on to serve the GWR until condemned during October 1879. Grange Court station was part of the Beeching closures in 1964.

Opposite and above **IRON DUKE CLASS –** *SULTAN* **AND** *TIMOUR*

For GWR express passenger services, Daniel Gooch designed the Iron Duke Class 4-2-2 in the mid-1840s. At this time, Swindon Works had just started building locomotives and the class was amongst the first engines erected there. The initial batch consisted of six, including *Sultan*, which is seen opposite, and the last in traffic from November 1847. A second order was placed soon after, consisting of 12 locomotives, and these were erected from June 1848 to June 1850. *Timour*, above, was completed during August 1849. A further four locomotives appeared from Swindon before the task was outsourced to Rothwell & Co. and the firm finished seven engines. The Iron Duke Class was active to the early 1870s when a start was made on rebuilding the locomotives, though this was in fact a replacement of components and reuse of the name. *Timour* was an early rebuild, being transformed during July 1873, whilst *Sultan* followed suit in September 1876. Both are pictured in their rebuilt form and continued in service to the end of Broad Gauge during 1892.

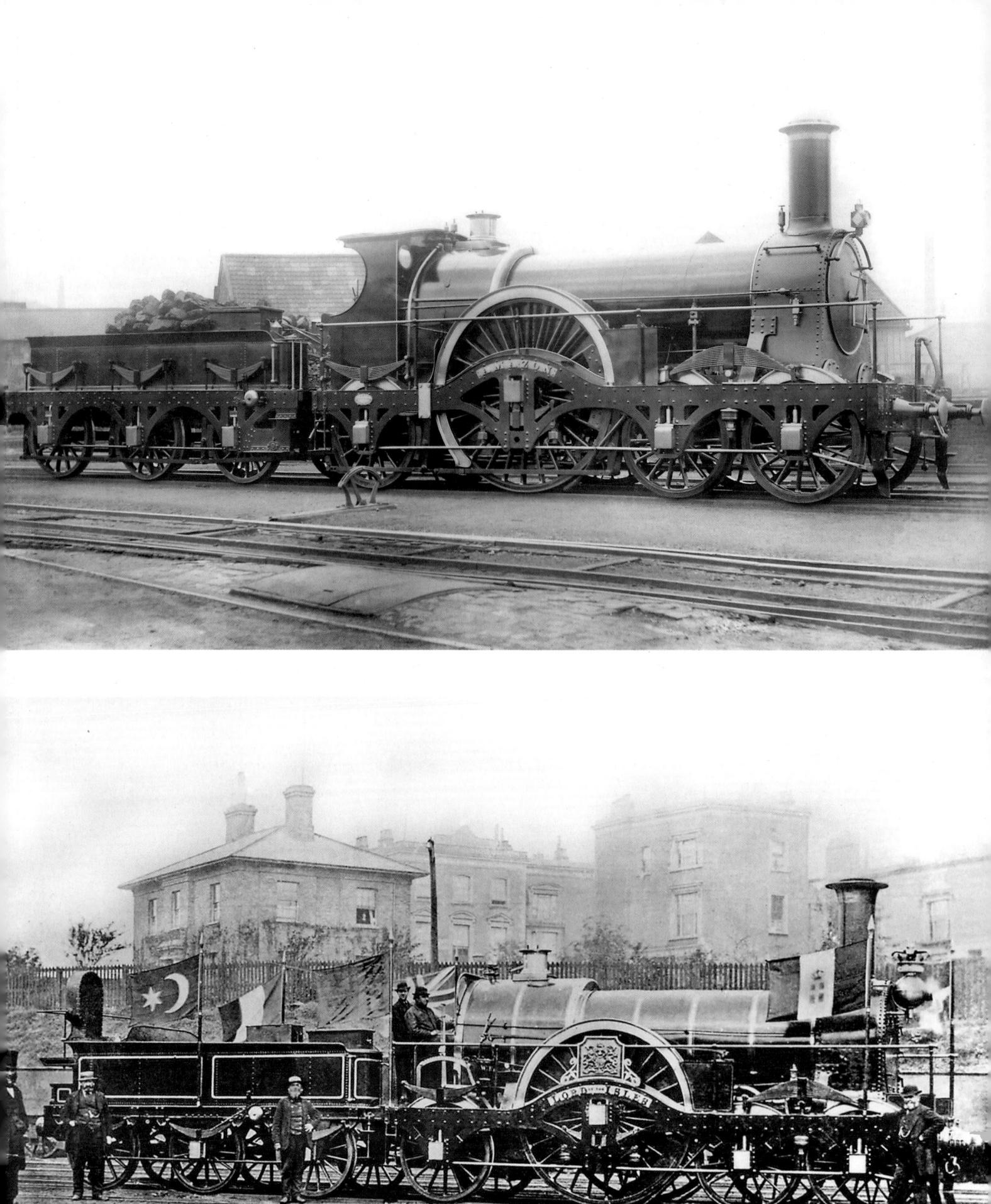

Above **IRON DUKE CLASS – *SEBASTOPOL***
The final seven Iron Duke Class 4-2-2 locomotives were erected between November 1854 and July 1855 by Rothwell & Co. of Bolton. Active from the 1820s, the firm was to be defunct in less than a decade. *Sebastopol* was the last locomotive from the order to be built in July 1855. As the group was built at the height of the Crimean War, the names were taken from notable engagements in the conflict. The engine was in service to October 1880 when rebuilt.

Opposite above **IRON DUKE CLASS – *AMAZON***
Iron Duke Class 4-2-2 *Amazon* was the penultimate class member to be constructed at Swindon in March 1851. Originally, the Iron Duke boiler had a heating surface of nearly 2,000 square feet and possessed a working pressure of 100 lb per sq. in., later raised to 115 lb per sq. in. When rebuilt, the boiler had a lower heating surface, which varied according to year of the transformation, but a higher pressure of 140 lb per sq. in. *Amazon* was a September 1878 rebuild and the heating surface of the boiler at this time was 1,727.8 sq. ft.

Opposite below **IRON DUKE CLASS – *LORD OF THE ISLES***
To the west of Paddington station at Westbourne Park, Iron Duke Class *Lord of the Isles* has been specially decorated to welcome the Brigade of Guards on their return from the Crimean War in 1856. The locomotive was the last of the Swindon-built group, entering traffic in March 1851. Soon after, *Lord of the Isles* was present at the Great Exhibition and made other appearances as a display piece for the GWR, such as at Edinburgh in 1890, the Chicago World's Fair in 1893 and the Victorian Era Exhibition at Earl's Court during 1897. Interestingly, the engine was not rebuilt and was withdrawn in June 1884, being stored to the early 20th century when scrapped.

Above **BRISTOL & EXETER RAILWAY 2-4-0 – NO. 2021**
Though initially operated by the GWR, the Bristol & Exeter Railway decided to handle their own locomotive affairs following the expiration of the original agreement. The influence of the GWR remained, however, and the B&ER ordered a version of the Iron Duke Class 4-2-2 locomotives in the late 1840s. In the 1870s, Locomotive Engineer James Pearson introduced a passenger 2-4-0 and a total of ten were erected at the company's workshops in Bristol. No. 2021 was produced in June 1871 as B&ER no. 43. The company was absorbed by the GWR in 1876, with no. 43 becoming stock no. 2021 and the engine was one of four class members to be active to the end of Broad Gauge.

Opposite above **DIDO CLASS – NO. 2151 *ARGO***
In the early 1860s four 0-6-0ST locomotives were procured from Slaughter, Grüning & Co. by both the South Devon Railway and Cornwall Railway, with the quartet split evenly between the two. A short time later, another four were built and distributed in the same manner. No. 2151 *Argo* was part of the second batch and went to the Cornwall Railway when completed by Slaughter, Grüning & Co. during 1863. At the time, the locomotive was only named and did not receive the number until taken into stock by the GWR when the company was absorbed in 1876. No. 2151 was in service to the end of Broad Gauge during 1892.

Opposite below **SHARP, STEWART & CO. 4-4-0ST – NO. 2135 *MAGPIE***
The Carmarthen & Cardigan Railway was an early enterprise to connect the two places, yet fell short of the aim owing to financial problems. Joining with the GWR-backed South Wales Railway at Carmarthen, when the line was converted to Standard Gauge in 1872 the C&CR had to follow suit. This displaced the company's Broad Gauge engines and some were sold to the South Devon Railway. The transaction included two Sharp, Stewart & Co. 4-4-0T locomotives which had been acquired in 1861. At the time of the purchase the pair was converted to saddle tanks and later transferred to GWR stock in 1876. *Magpie* was one of the pair and became GWR no. 2135, being in service with name and number to the late 1880s. The other locomotive was *Heron*, no. 2134, which survived to the Broad Gauge conversion.

Above **IRON DUKE CLASS 4-2-2 – *TORNADO***
Despite the impending demise of the Broad Gauge, Gooch built three final 4-2-2 locomotives in 1888. The last was *Tornado* which took the name from withdrawn Iron Duke Class engine *Tornado*, operational between 1849 and 1881. The new *Tornado* was in service just four years until 1892.

Opposite above **IRON DUKE CLASS – *IRON DUKE***
A group has posed with 4-2-2 *Iron Duke* in the late 19th century. Built at Swindon during April 1847, the engine's first career lasted to October 1871. The nominal rebuild emerged in August 1873 and continued in traffic to the end of the Broad Gauge.

Opposite below **BRISTOL & EXETER RAILWAY 4-2-2 – NO. 2008**
The Bristol & Exeter Railway was inspired by the success of the Iron Duke Class to introduce a similar express locomotive, though with 7 ft 6 in. diameter driving wheels instead of 8 ft. A total of 20 were produced by Stothert, Slaughter & Co. in 1849. By the time of amalgamation with the GWR, 12 had been withdrawn, but B&ER no. 9 was still in service and became GWR no. 2008, performing for the company to 1889.

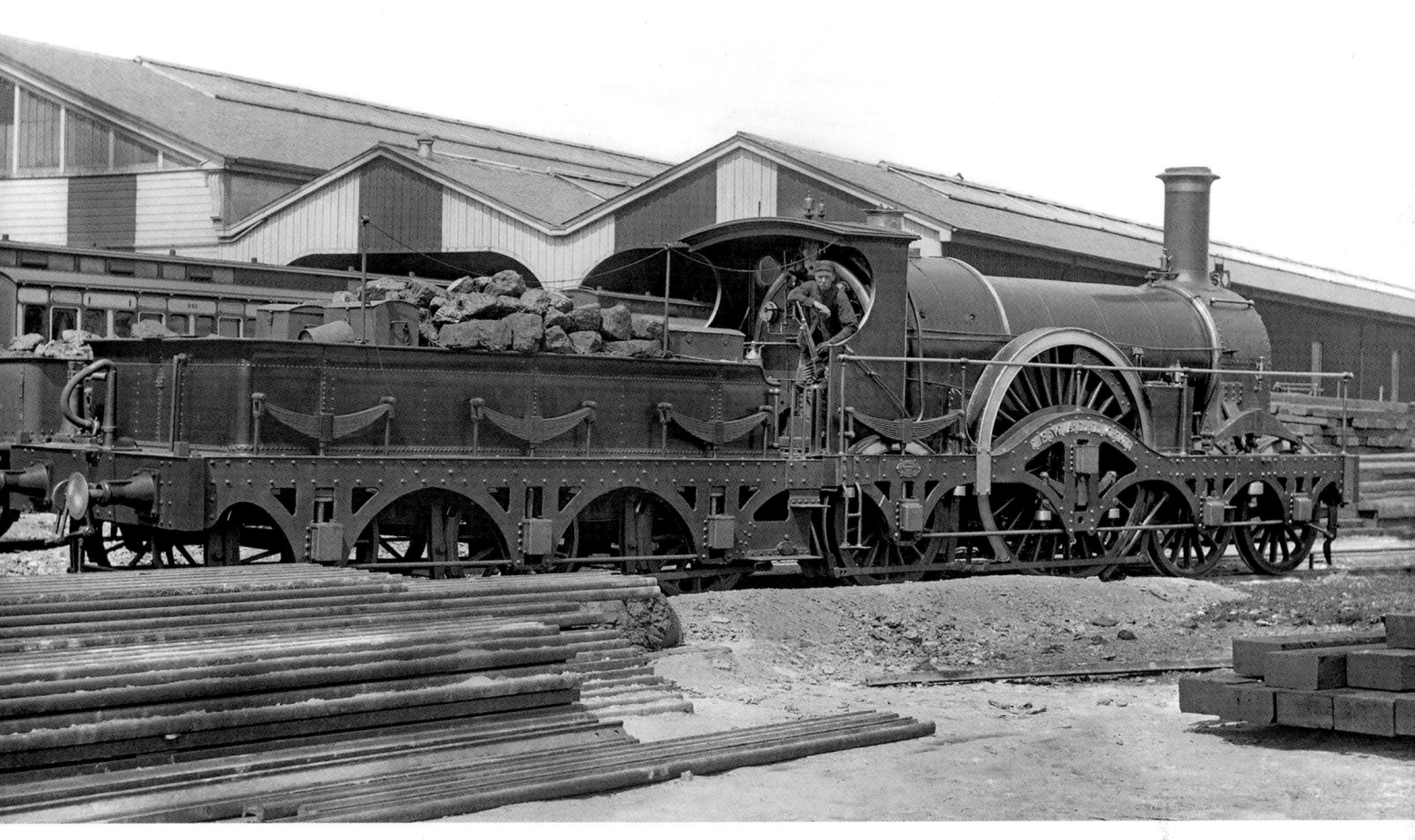

Above **IRON DUKE CLASS 4-2-2 – SWALLOW**
Westbourne Park shed was a short distance away from Paddington station to the west. Established in 1855, the stabling area was increased in the 1860s and both were in use until 1906 with the completion of Old Oak Common depot. In the late 1880s, Iron Duke Class 4-2-2 *Swallow* is at Westbourne Park for servicing. The locomotive was the second class member to be rebuilt in September 1871, following *Rover* a month earlier, and continued in traffic to the end of Broad Guage. Photograph from the David P. Williams Archive.

Opposite **DEAN 3001 CLASS 2-2-2 – NO. 3023**
With the demise of Broad Gauge gaining momentum in the 1870s, GWR Locomotive Engineer Joseph Armstrong thought of the subsequent conversion possibilities for new locomotives both to and from Standard Gauge. His successor, William Dean, was also mindful of the issue and as late as 1891 eight new Broad Gauge 2-2-2s were built ready for conversion to Standard Gauge around a year later. One of this number was no. 3023 and the locomotive has been pictured in the brief period from construction in July 1891 to July 1892 when rebuilt. The engine has posed with crew at Westbourne Park shed, to the west of Paddington station. Photograph from the David P. Williams Archive courtesy Rail-Online.

Above **3521 CLASS 4-4-0 – NO. 3540**
A number of passenger tank engines appeared in the late 1880s to a design which had both Standard and Broad Gauge versions. These were initially 0-4-2T locomotives for Standard and 0-4-2ST for Broad, yet unsteadiness affected the running and soon after the wheel arrangement was changed to 0-4-4T for all. Problems persisted and at the turn of the century the locomotives became 4-4-0s with a tender. No. 3540 was the last of the Standard Gauge 0-4-2Ts built in 1889 and modified three years later. The locomotive was rebuilt as a 4-4-0 in 1900 and received a Standard No. 3 boiler, whilst a number also received Standard No. 2 boilers. No. 3540 has been caught at Bristol Bath Road station around 1901. The engine survived to November 1927. Photograph from Rail Archive Stephenson courtesy Rail-Online.

Opposite above **3001 CLASS 4-2-2 – NO. 3023**
An express is at Bath Spa station in the mid-1900s with Dean 3001 Class 4-2-2 no. 3023 *Swallow*. Starting life as a 2-2-2, instability at the front end caused the class to be rebuilt as a 4-2-2 in the mid-1890s. No. 3023 was converted in September 1894. The locomotive has also subsequently acquired the name of withdrawn Iron Duke Class 4-2-2 *Swallow*. Photograph from Rail Archive Stephenson courtesy Rail-Online.

Opposite below **3001 CLASS 4-2-2 – NO. 3023**
Originally intended for South West England expresses, the 3001 Class 4-2-2s were displaced as the 20th century progressed and new work was found on the Birmingham and Wolverhampton line. Latterly, the engines were used on the Worcester and Oxford lines, as well as local services between London and Bristol. No. 3023 *Swallow* is seen in the yard at Old Oak Common shed c. 1910. The locomotive was condemned during 1912. Photograph from Rail Archive Stephenson courtesy Rail-Online.

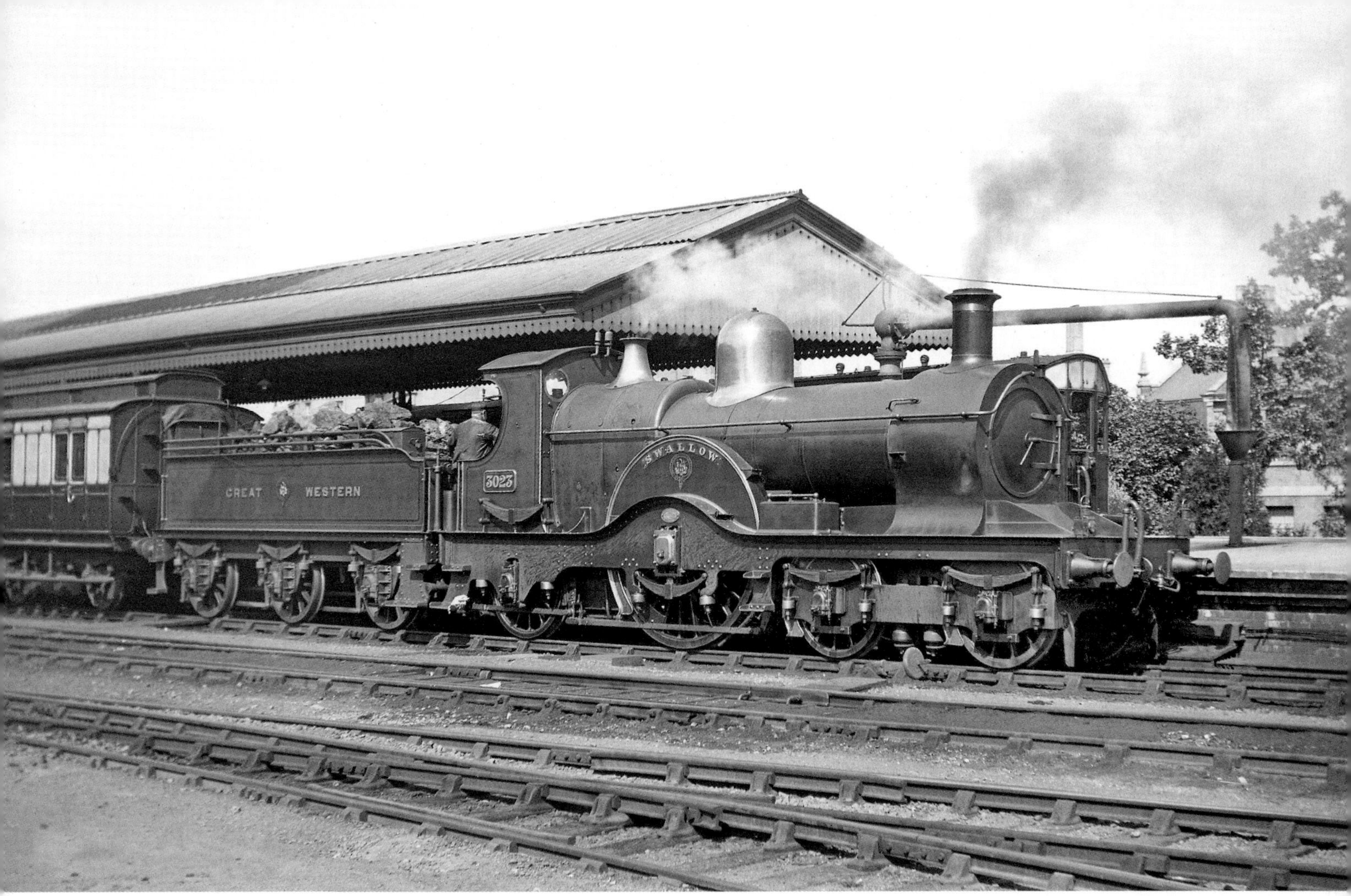
GREAT WESTERN
3023
SWALLOW

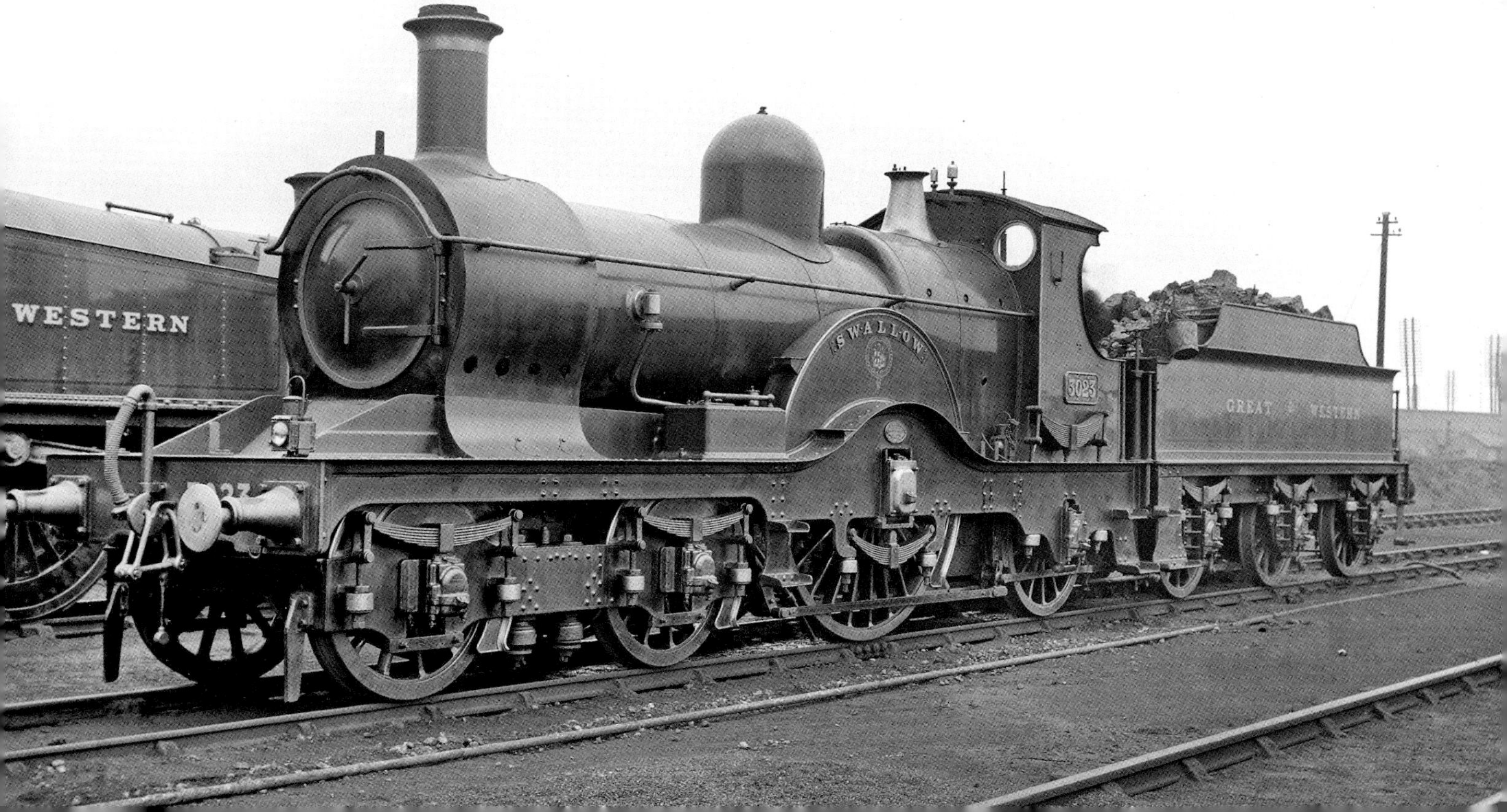
WESTERN
SWALLOW
3023
GREAT WESTERN

Above BROAD GAUGE LOCOMOTIVES
Although the end of Broad Gauge had been signalled in the early 1870s, the situation persisted to the weekend of 21st and 22nd May 1892 when the final conversion took place. At this time there were 177 miles of track to realign and this was carried out by 4,000 men, with a cost of around £800,000. Most of the rolling stock recently built was capable of conversion to Standard Gauge and approx. 130 locomotives and 430 carriages were so treated to the mid-1890s. Dedicated sidings had to be laid at Swindon to store the stock as the process was carried out and many are seen here in the yard.

Opposite above 79 CLASS 0-6-0 – NO. 123
As the GWR expanded by purchasing other railways, the company was presented with Standard Gauge stock. In the mid-1850s, the Shrewsbury & Chester Railway was taken over and the company's workshops became the centre for the GWR's Standard Gauge operation, which was overseen by Joseph Armstrong for a time before he became Locomotive Carriage and Wagon Superintendent. One of Daniel Gooch's early Standard Gauge designs was the 57 Class 0-6-0 of 1855. Soon after this was developed with smaller wheels and larger cylinders, with these engines forming the 79 Class. No. 123 was part of the group and appeared in traffic during December 1861. A number of the 79 Class locomotives were rebuilt in the late 1870s, early 1880s with saddle tanks and no. 123 was converted during December 1879. The engine saw further rebuilding in October 1920 with pannier tanks. This kept the locomotive in service to November 1927.

Opposite below 360 CLASS 0-6-0 – NO. 360
In 1864, Joseph Armstrong succeeded Daniel Gooch and one of his early designs in the position was the 360 Class 0-6-0. Twelve were constructed at Swindon in 1866, with no. 360 the first to be completed during April. Many were employed in the Northern Division and no. 360 was engaged there until December 1918.

STANDARD GAUGE LOCOMOTIVES – PRE-GROUPING

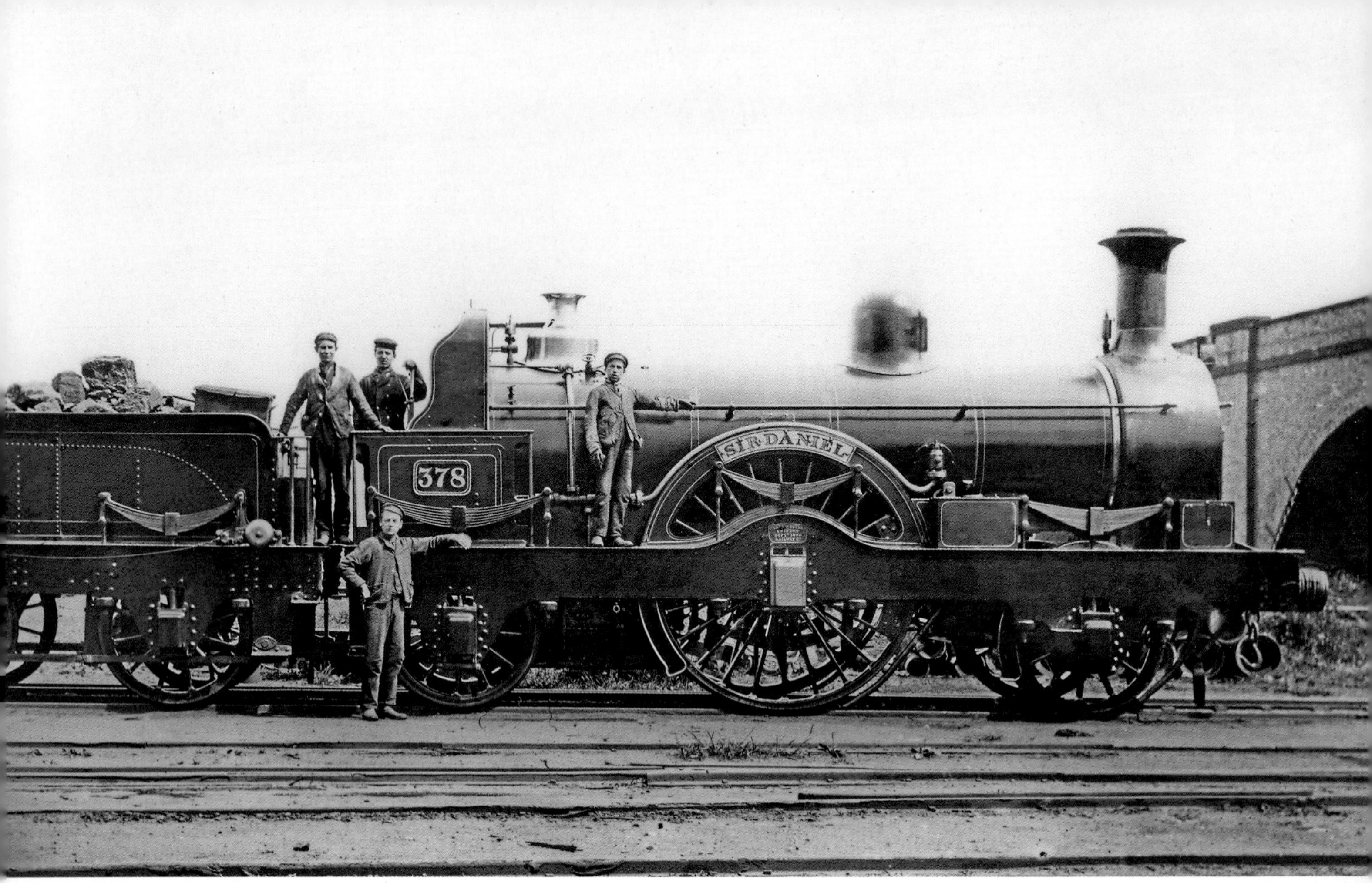
SIR DANIEL
378

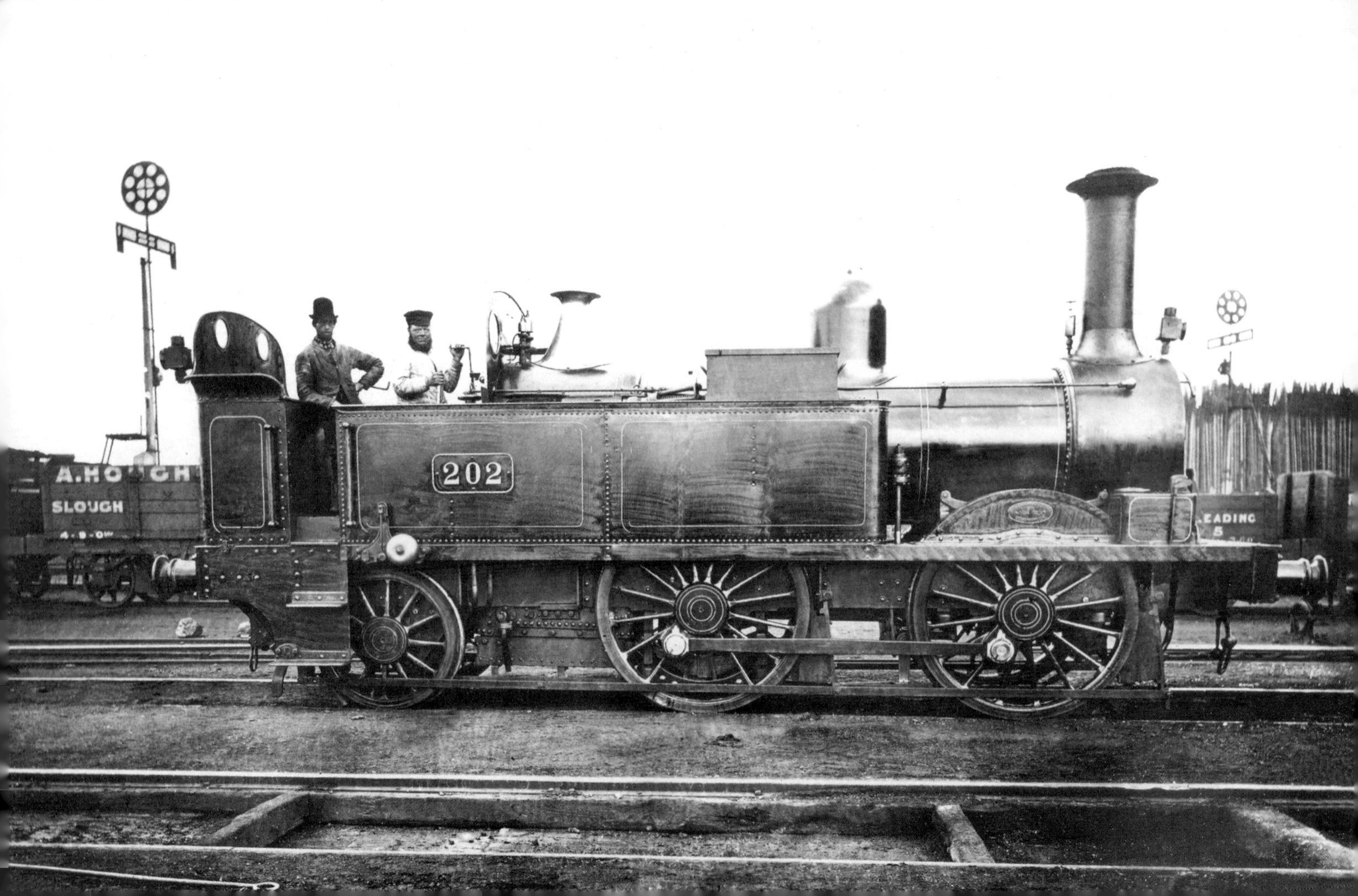
SLOUGH
202

Above **455 CLASS 2-4-0T – NO. 632**
Introduced for London suburban services and those running on the Metropolitan Railway lines, the 455 Class 2-4-0T, or 'Metro Tanks', saw 140 engines built with several variations over 30 years. No. 455 was in traffic from 1869 and no. 3500 marked the final appearance during 1899. No. 632 was an early example and constructed at Swindon in October 1871. The locomotive had a long service life, lasting to November 1929. Though many mainly worked in London, as time progressed the class spread out across the system.

Opposite above **378 CLASS 2-2-2 – NO. 378**
Joseph Armstrong's 378 or Sir Daniel Class 2-2-2 locomotives had the distinction of being the first Standard Gauge passenger engines to be completed at Swindon Works. Introduced in 1866, no. 378 *Sir Daniel* was the pioneer when completed in September and nine more followed before further lots appeared in the second half of 1869 bringing the total to 30. The locomotives were initially in the Northern Division before spreading with Standard Gauge. Active to around the turn of the century, seven members were condemned whilst the other 23 were rebuilt as 0-6-0s which extended their life to varying periods. All had gone to the scrapyard before Grouping. No. 378 *Sir Daniel* was the first class casualty when condemned in May 1898.

Opposite below **517 CLASS 0-4-2T – NO. 202**
The 517 Class 0-4-2T was first built at Wolverhampton in 1868 and thereafter evolved a diverse group of engines numbering 156 examples. No. 202 was completed in April 1876 and was in service to September 1928.

Above **455 CLASS 2-4-0T – NO. 1415**
Caught at Paddington station is 455 Class 2-4-0T no. 1415. The locomotive was one of a number of class members fitted for auto-train working in the 1920s/1930s, acquiring the apparatus in January 1930 and remaining so to withdrawal during 1938.

Below **BRISTOL & EXETER RAILWAY 0-6-0 – NO. 116**
No. 116 was built for the Bristol & Exeter Railway by Sharp, Stewart & Co. in 1875 as the first of a batch of ten locomotives. Renumbered 1366 by the GWR, the company also rebuilt the engine in May 1896. This kept the locomotive active to January 1907.

Above **1016 CLASS 0-6-0ST – NO. 1040**
Eleven of the 60 1016 Class 0-6-0ST locomotives were converted to pannier tanks in the early 20th century. No. 1040, built in May 1870, was amongst this number, also avoiding being superheated. Despite this, the engine was in service to January 1929.

Below **56 CLASS 2-4-0 – NO. 725**
Just 11 engines formed the 56 Class 2-4-0 which was designed by Joseph Armstrong in the early 1870s. No. 725 was the penultimate class member in traffic during September 1872.

Above **2361 CLASS 0-6-0 – NO. 2370**
In the mid-1880s, William Dean produced the designs for an 0-6-0 Class, unusually with outside frames and springs. A total of 20 were built in 1885 and 1886. No. 2370 appeared halfway in December 1885 and had a lifespan of 50 years. As part of the class's superheating programme, no. 2370 was modified just after Grouping.

Opposite above **3201 CLASS 2-4-0 – NO. 3203**
No. 3203 was originally one of five 3201 Class 2-4-0s built at Swindon in 1884/1885. At this time, these locomotives shared a similar design to other Dean classes, with outside frames, springs, etc., including convertible 2-4-0s built for the Broad Gauge and a 2-4-0T version was also placed in traffic. At the end of the Broad Gauge, those locomotives joined the 3201 Class and the 2-4-0Ts were converted to tender locomotives. No. 3203 was in traffic to August 1925.

Opposite below **2301 CLASS 0-6-0 – NO. 2325**
Over 16 years, Swindon Works produced 260 2301, or 'Dean Goods', 0-6-0s. No. 2325 was an early example, being completed during February 1884.

Above 2301 CLASS 0-6-0 – NO. 2383

Built in June 1890, 2301 Class no. 2383 was one of a number of class members that went on to serve the British Army during the First World War. Over 60 were taken to France in 1917 and repatriated around 1919, though several saw further service and a small group ultimately never came back. Some engines also served in the Second World War, yet no. 2838 remained on home soil and saw the end of the conflict, being withdrawn during August 1946.

Opposite above 3031 CLASS 4-2-2 – NO. 3033

Following in the footsteps of the 3001 Class 2-2-2s, the 3031 Class was similar but the engines were constructed new with a bogie whereas the earlier locomotives saw a conversion programme carried out. No. 3033 *Albatross* was the third of the 3031 Class built at Swindon Works in July 1894. The engine has an express here at Oxford during the short service life of just 15 years.

Opposite below 7 CLASS 4-4-0 – NO. 7

Dean experimented with compound locomotives in the mid-1880s which proved to be unsuccessful. Two of these, no. 7 and no. 8, were nominally rebuilt to form part of a small class of 4-4-0s built in 1894. No. 7 appeared in March and was originally named *Charles Saunders* but was subsequently changed to *Armstrong*. Work was found for the locomotives on the line from London to Bristol and later in the Midlands. Despite the 7 Class 4-4-0s being few in number, they were superheated in the early 1910s and were in service past Grouping to 1928-1930 when condemned. No. 7 left traffic in September 1928.

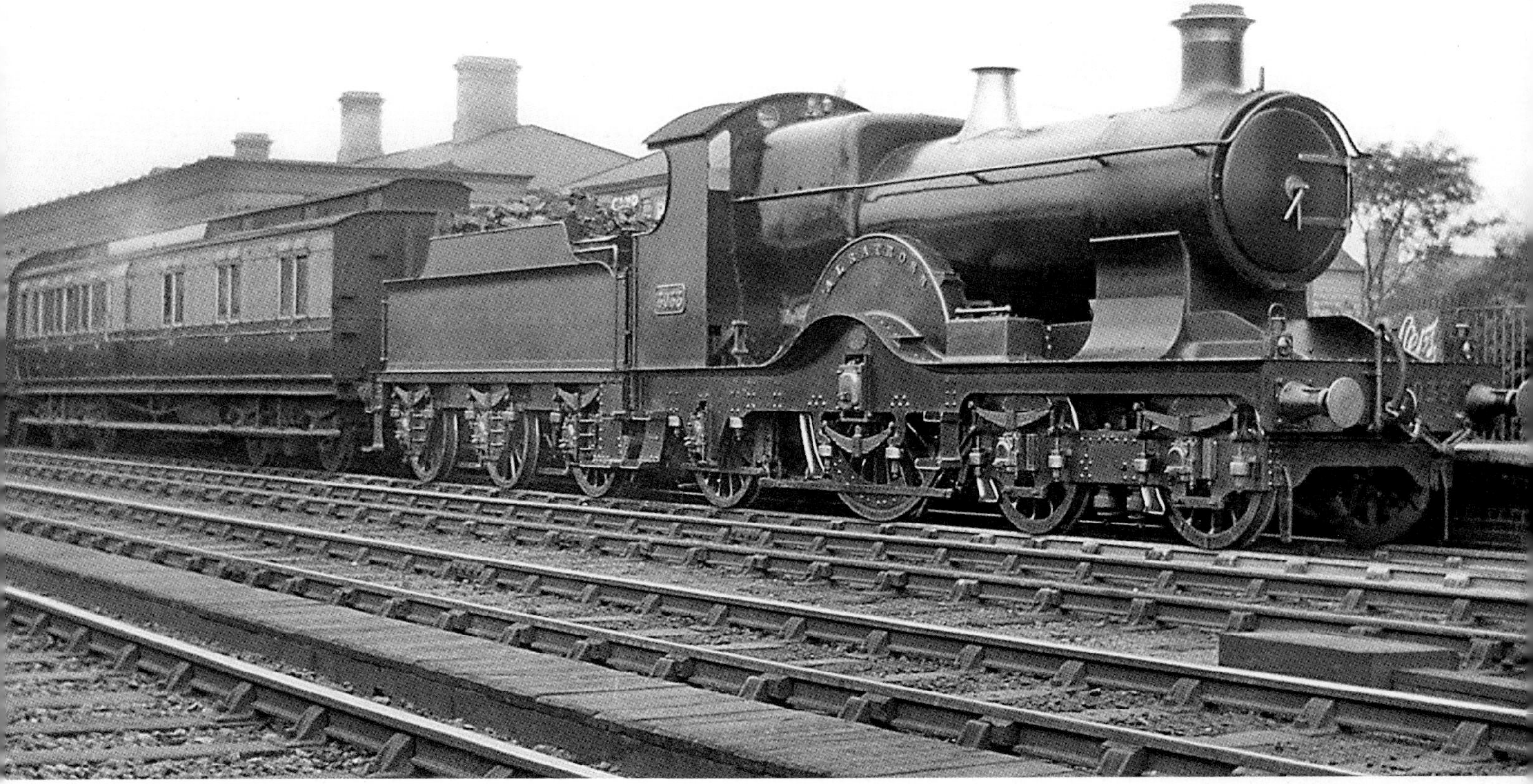

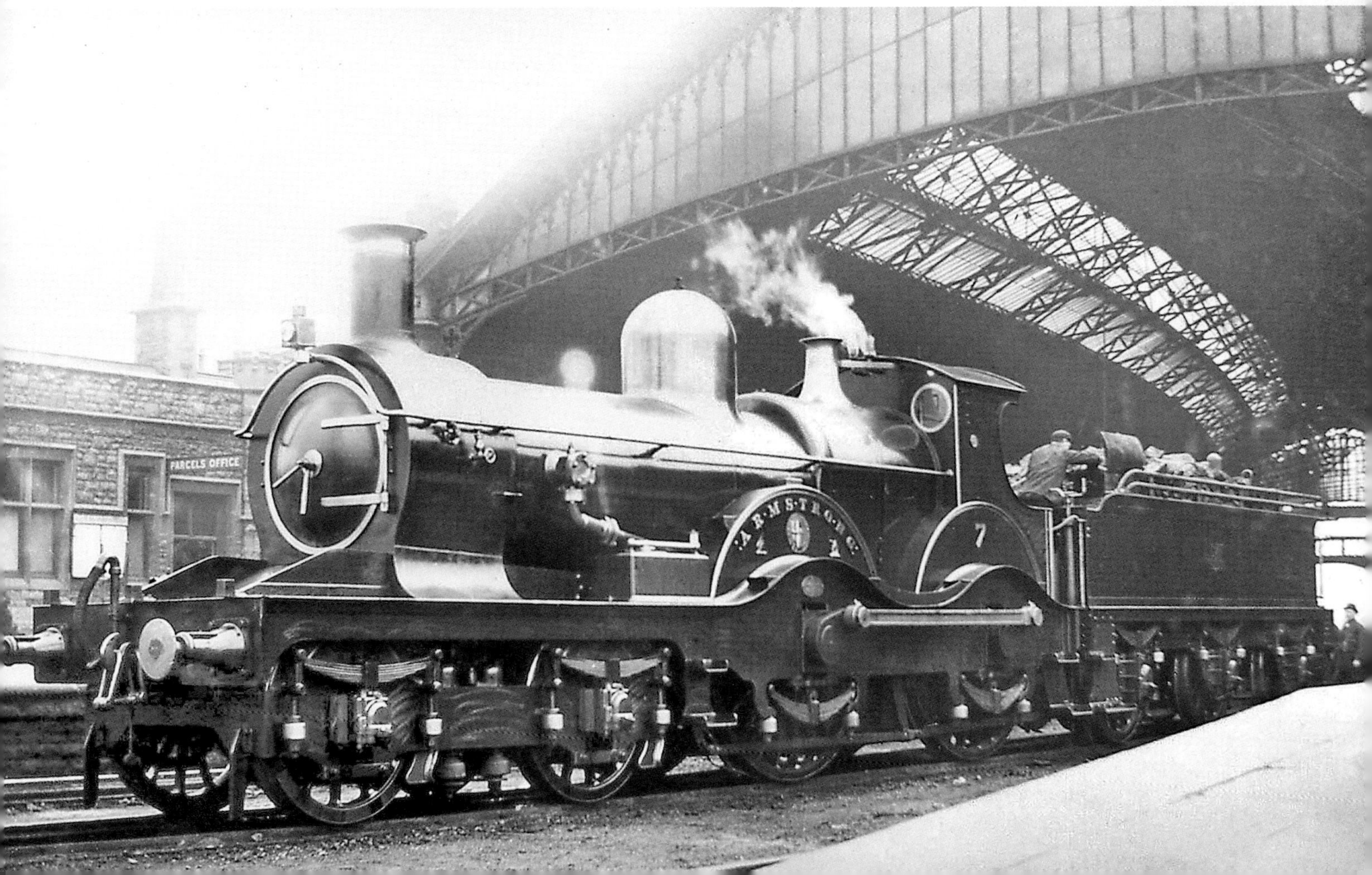
PARCELS OFFICE
ARMSTRONG
7

Above **2301 CLASS 0-6-0 – NO. 2515**
Though the 2301 Class was generally similar, there existed variations in boiler type used. Starting with domeless boilers, some class members soon had a dome on the front boiler ring before the diameter was increased 2 in. for a large group. The remaining 2301 Class engines had the dome placed on the rear boiler ring which is the case here for no. 2515. Erected in March 1897, no. 2515 was new with the type and another feature of difference with other class members was the fitting of fluted coupling rods. In this image, these have been replaced with plain rods. No. 2515 was in service to February 1953.

Opposite above **3252 CLASS 4-4-0 – NO. 3265**
For duties in the far West Country, Dean designed a 4-4-0 and 60 appeared from Swindon in the last four years of the 19th century. Most of these engines had a round-top firebox but the last examples had Belpaire fireboxes. Subsequently a number of 3252 Class members had the type fitted. No. 3265 *Tre Pol and Pen* was new with the first type in July 1896 and changed in January 1905. The locomotive was in service to December 1929 when rebuilt as a prototype for the 3200 Class 4-4-0.

Opposite below **69 CLASS 2-4-0 – NO. 74**
A small number of 2-2-2s were nominally rebuilt under Dean at Swindon in the late 19th century. The 69, or River, Class 2-4-0 was the result and comprised eight locomotives. No. 74 *Stour* was new in March 1897 and had a short career lasting to December 1918.

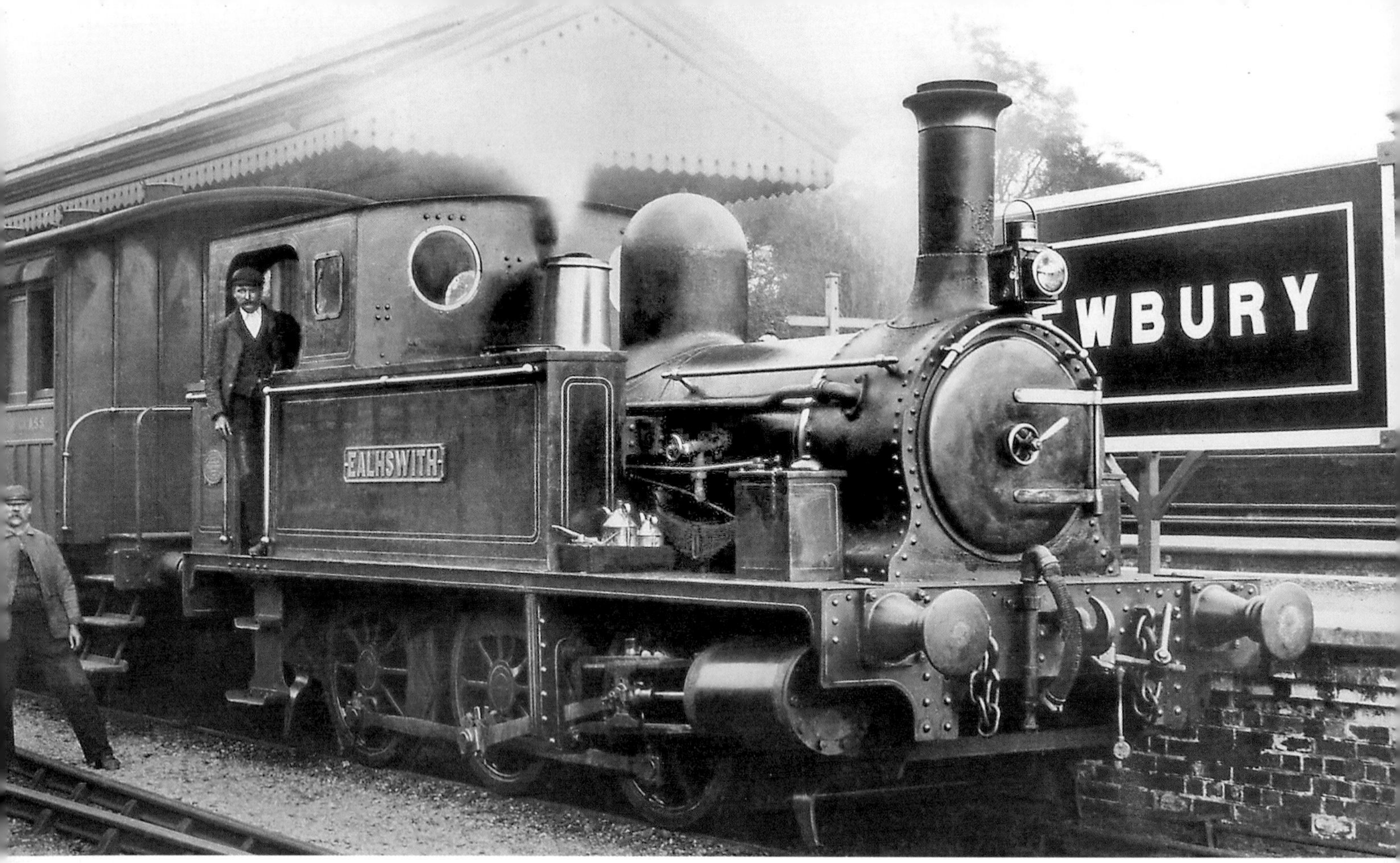
WBURY
EALHSWITH

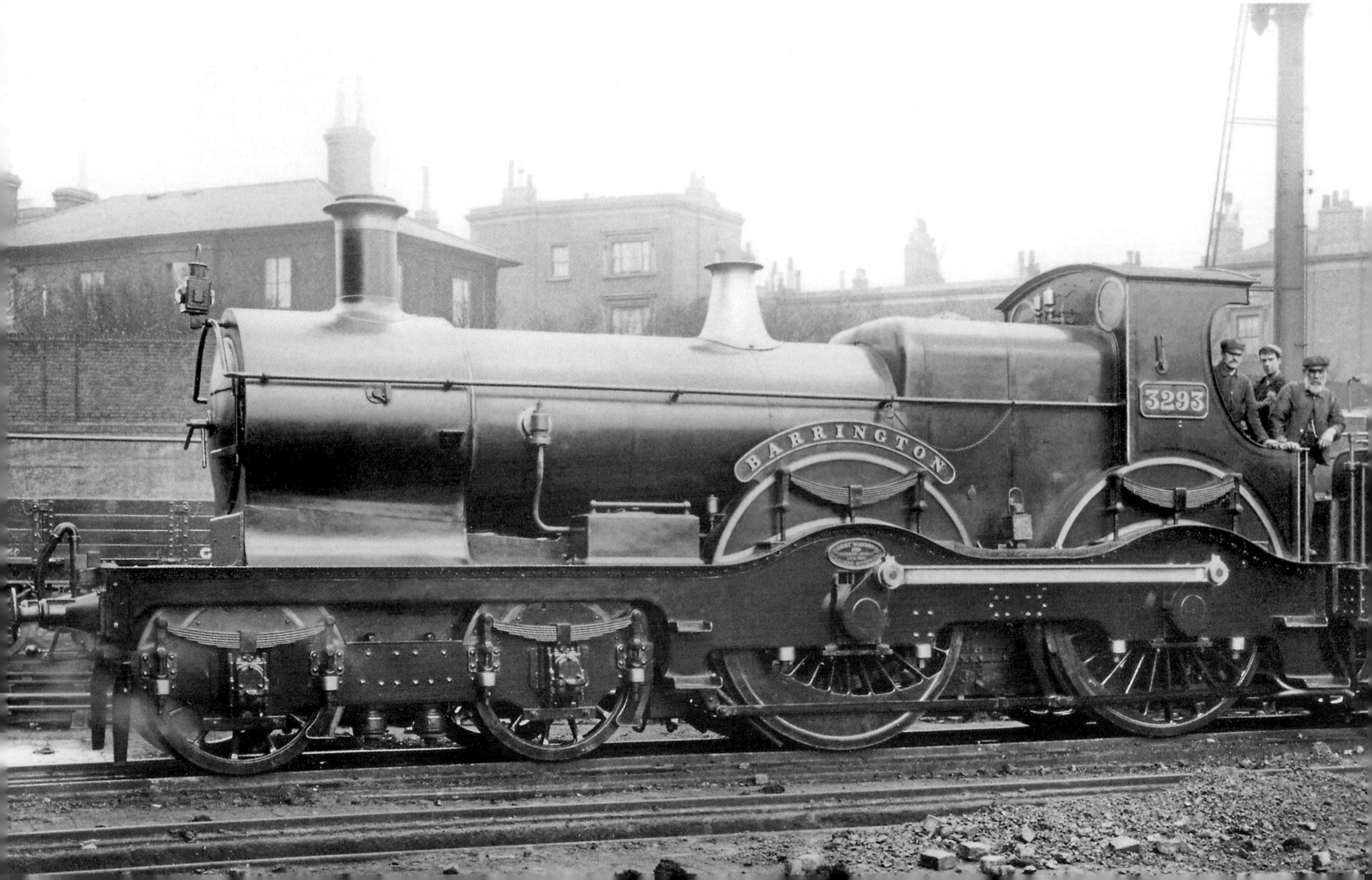
BARRINGTON
3293

Above **1901 CLASS 0-6-0ST – NO. 2020**
The 1901 Class 0-6-0ST was originally a separate entity owing to the position of the dome on the boiler. In this instance, the dome was placed centrally. The earlier 850 Class had the dome positioned over the firebox, yet when a reboilering programme involving the pair started in 1910, also seeing the saddle tank replaced with pannier tanks, the earlier classification was favoured and the 1901 engines were reclassified. No. 2020 was the last 1901 Class 0-6-0ST built to George Armstrong's design at Wolverhampton during May 1895. The locomotive was rebuilt in October 1923 and continued in traffic to December 1938. At this time, no. 2020 was sold to a colliery at Ammanford, South Wales.

Opposite above **LAMBOURN VALLEY RAILWAY 0-6-0T –** *EALHSWITH*
On the line from Reading to Hungerford, Newbury station opened in late 1847. Before the end of the century, this point was the junction for the light railway branch to Lambourn. Initially operated by the GWR, the LVR bought two locomotives from Chapman & Furneaux, Gateshead in 1898. These were 0-6-0T engines and one, *Ealhswith*, stands at Newbury station here. Their association with the route was brief, however, as the Cambrian Railways bought the two in 1904. The pair was taken into GWR stock just before Grouping and in service for almost a decade before sold to industry. The LVR was absorbed by the GWR and remained open to passengers until 1960.

Opposite below **3292 CLASS 4-4-0 – NO. 3293**
Between 1897 and 1899, Dean introduced 20 3292 Class 4-4-0s for the London to Bristol service. A notable feature included in the design at this time was the Belpaire firebox. No. 3293 *Barrington* was the second class member from Swindon in May 1898. The engine is pictured at Westbourne Park.

Above **3300 CLASS 4-4-0 – NO. 3346**
No. 3346 of the 3300 Class poses with a rake of clerestory carriages in the early 20th century. Photograph from Rail Archive Stephenson courtesy Rail-Online.

Opposite **3000 CLASS 4-2-2 – NO. 3030**
The last 3000 Class locomotive was no. 3030 *Westward Ho* built in December 1891. Rebuilt as a 4-2-2 in October 1894, the engine was in traffic to May 1909. During the first years of the 20th century, no. 3030 has been pictured emerging from Parsons Tunnel, Dawlish, with a local train to Newton Abbot. Photograph by Robert Brookman from Rail Archive Stephenson courtesy Rail-Online.

Below **2300 CLASS 0-6-0 – NO. 2322**
Activity has paused for 2300 Class no. 2322 to be pictured in the early 20th century.

Above **ATBARA CLASS 4-4-0 – NO. 3378**
At the start of the 20th century the Atbara Class 4-4-0 was built for express passenger traffic across the system. This role was cut short by the introduction of the 4000 Class 4-6-0s and other engines as time progressed. No. 3378 *Khartoum* was built in May 1900 and is seen at Newton Abbot within the first decade of service. Withdrawals occurred over just a few years, starting in the late 1920s. No. 3378 was the first to be condemned in this period, going in April 1927. Photograph by Robert Brookman from Rail Archive Stephenson courtesy Rail-Online.

Opposite above **CHURCHWARD DE GLEHN COMPOUND 4-4-2 – NO. 104**
Towards the end of the 19th century locomotive engineers looked to compound working for improvements in the efficiency of the steam locomotive. This meant several sets of cylinders were used to obtain the most amount of work from the steam as possible. In many instances, two sets of two cylinders were fitted – one set working at high pressure and the other one low. De Glehn designed a successful system for railways in France and this was adopted by other engineers. When G.J. Churchward became Chief Mechanical Engineer of the GWR in 1902, he decided to experiment with the arrangement and a 4-4-2 was obtained from Société Alsacienne de Constructions Mécaniques in France. Arriving in Britain during 1903, no. 102 *La France* was tested before another two locomotives were built in 1905. No. 104 *Alliance* was the last of the pair which were slightly larger than no. 102. The trio appear to have been satisfactory but without significant advantage over the GWR design practices of the time, though much greater success was found with compounds in Europe and America. Nevertheless, the trio was kept in employment to the late 1920s, with no. 104 the last to be condemned during September 1928.

Opposite below **4000 CLASS 4-6-0 – NO. 4012**
In order to offer a true comparison between compound and simple expansion, Churchward built his own four-cylinder 4-4-2 locomotive in 1906. No. 40, later no. 4000 soon proved more suitable and was selected for development. A 4-6-0 wheel arrangement was thought desirable for power and adhesion and used for the new locomotives. The first ten built in 1907 were named after stars. The second group of ten were given names of orders of chivalry. No. 4012 *Knight of the Thistle* was part of the batch and in service from March 1908. The cab of the engine is recorded in this image.

Above **3000 CLASS 4-2-2 – NO. 3026**
Leaving Teignmouth with an eastbound express in 1903 is 3000 Class no. 3026 *Tornado*. Photograph by Robert Brookman from Rail Archive Stephenson courtesy Rail-Online.

Opposite above **CHURCHWARD 4-6-2 PACIFIC – NO. 111 *THE GREAT BEAR***
No. 111 *The Great Bear* had the distinction of being the first 4-6-2 Pacific locomotive to be constructed for a British railway. The design appears to have been no more than an experiment by Churchward and the locomotive was rebuilt as a 4-6-0 in 1924.

Opposite below **3521 CLASS 4-4-0 – NO. 3525**
Paused at Slough station with a local train in 1902 is 3521 Class no. 3525. Photograph by Robert Brookman from Rail Archive Stephenson courtesy Rail-Online.

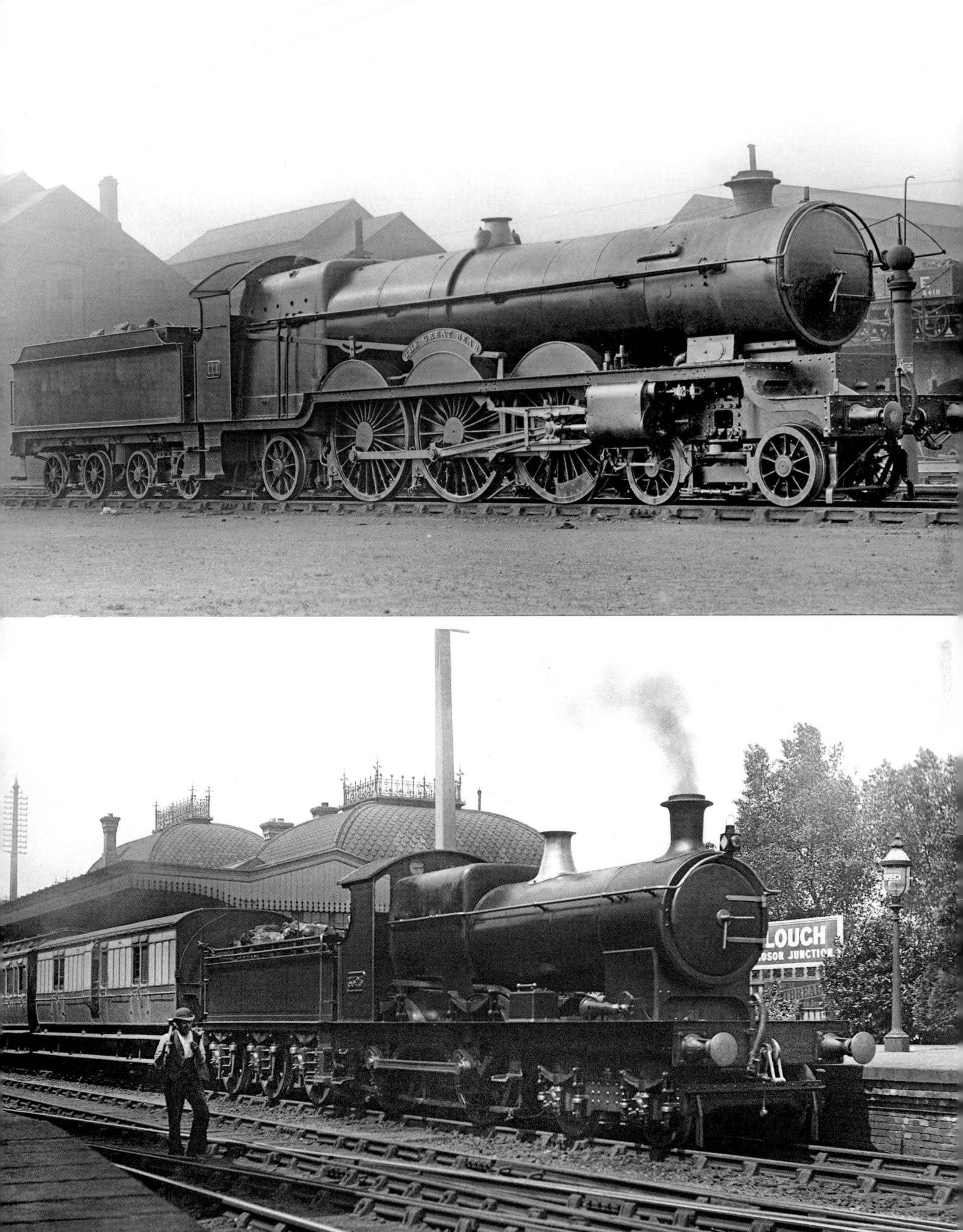

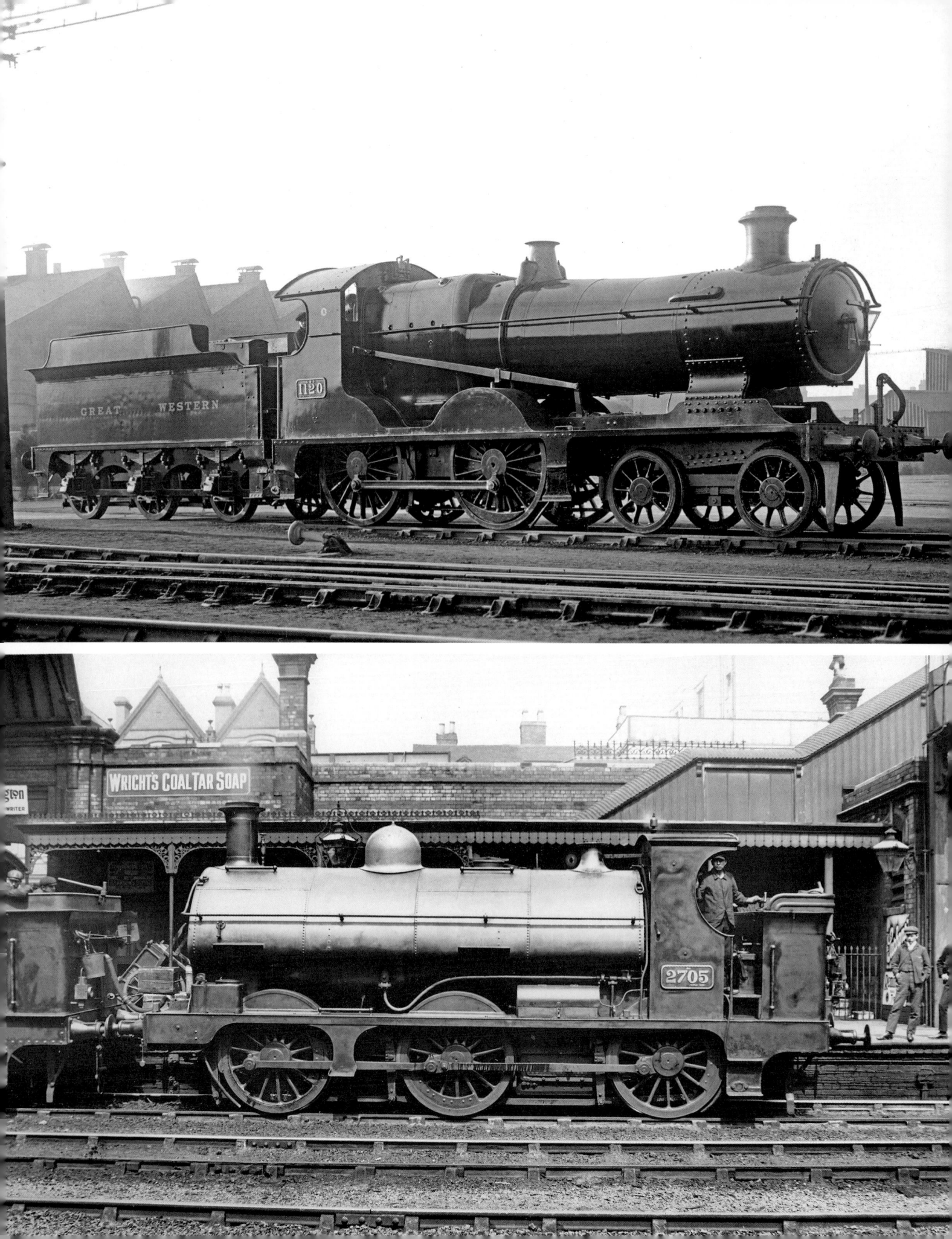

Above **3031 CLASS 4-2-2 – NO. 3047**
In the early 20th century, 3031 Class no. 3047 *Lorna Doone* poses for the camera. The locomotive was new in February 1895 and ran to November 1912 when withdrawn. Photograph from Rail Archive Stephenson courtesy Rail-Online.

Opposite above **MIDLAND & SOUTH WESTERN JUNCTION 4-4-0 – NO. 1120**
From near Cheltenham, the Midland & South Western Junction Railway operated sixty miles of lines connecting with the London & South Western Railway at Andover. The M&SWJR held a small group of nearly 30 locomotives which the GWR took over at Grouping in 1923. Amongst these were nine 4-4-0s built from 1905 to 1914 by the North British Locomotive Company to a design supplied by M&SWJR Locomotive Superintendent James Tyrrell. No. 2 was built in 1909 and became GWR no. 1120 at Grouping and later acquired a GWR Standard No. 2 boiler in 1928. Yet this was not enough to keep the locomotive employed and no. 1120 was the first of the group to be withdrawn during August 1931. The engine is seen with the GWR boiler here.

Opposite below **655 CLASS 0-6-0ST – NO. 2705**
George Armstrong produced the design for the 655 Class 0-6-0ST in 1892 and to the second half of the decade 52 examples were constructed. No. 2705 was erected as part of the final order for 20 and ready for work in March 1896. The engine is pictured at Wolverhampton in the early 20th century. Fitted with a new boiler and pannier tanks during 1920, no. 2705 was in traffic to February 1945. Photograph by Robert Brookman from Rail Archive Stephenson courtesy Rail-Online.

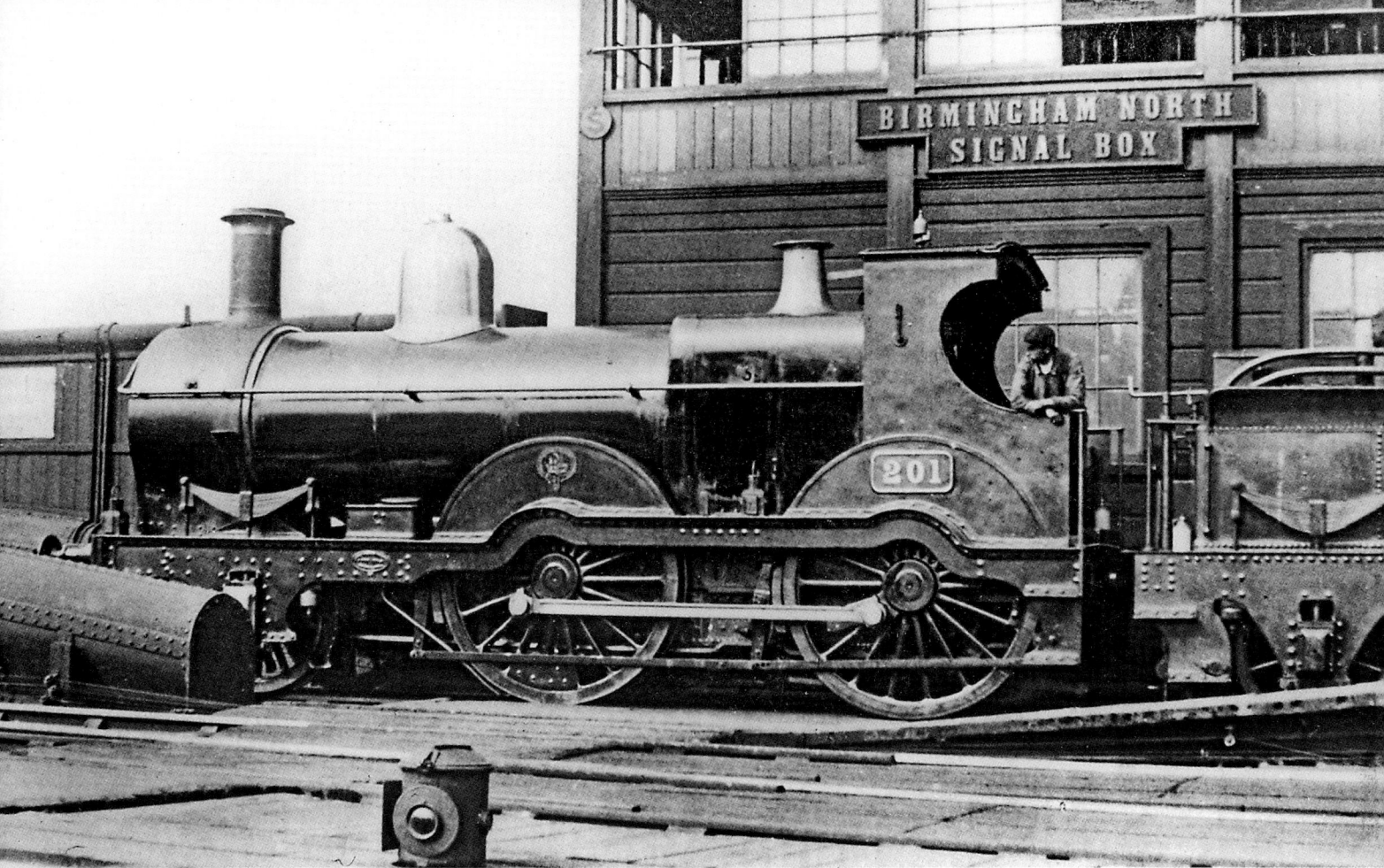

Above **196 CLASS 2-4-0 – NO. 201**
Beyer, Peacock & Co. delivered a number of 2-2-2 express engines to the West Midland Railway in 1861. The manufacturers also produced several 2-4-0s for the company at the time. No. 201, which is seen at Birmingham Snow Hill station in the early 20th century, was amongst this latter group. Originally WMR no. 111, the locomotive was rebuilt as a 2-4-0T in February 1879, yet this transformation was short-lived and by the mid-1880s the engine was returned to a 2-4-0 tender arrangement. From this time, no. 201 worked in the Northern Division to May 1917. Photograph courtesy Rail-Online.

Opposite above **3300 CLASS 4-4-0 – NO. 3434**
The 3300 Class 4-4-0 was introduced in 1899 and built up to 1910. During this process, the boiler used evolved from a parallel domeless example to a domeless taper type. The penultimate batch of 15 locomotives was completed in 1906 and included no. 3434 *Joseph Shaw*, pictured. At this time the number was 3724 and a name was not used. The first change was the number to 3434 as part of the 1912 scheme whilst the name was present from 1917. During July 1937, the locomotive was condemned.

Opposite below **3800 CLASS 4-4-0 – NO. 3828**
In 1904, Churchward constructed the first 3800 Class 4-4-0. Over the next eight years a total of 40 were completed with all named after British Counties, as well as those in Ireland. No. 3828 *County of Hereford* was erected in January 1912 and new with a superheater fitted. The locomotive was in traffic to March 1933 and is seen here at Beaconsfield station before the First World War.

Above **3800 CLASS 4-4-0 – NO. 3818**
The Churchward 3800 Class had the distinction of being the last 4-4-0s built new for the GWR, whilst also being the company's only outside cylinder engine with the wheel arrangement. No. 3818 *County of Radnor* was built in December 1906 and used a superheated boiler from October 1910. The locomotive was in service to August 1931. No. 3818 has a train for Bristol at Weston-super-Mare station, c. 1910. Photograph from Rail Archive Stephenson courtesy Rail-Online.

Opposite above and below **SWINDON WORKS**
Before the establishment of the railways, Swindon was a market town of around 2,500 persons. Early on, the Great Western Railway, particularly Isambard Kingdom Brunel and Daniel Gooch, recognised the need to establish suitable facilities for servicing locomotives. The site chosen was around one mile north of Swindon in open country which left ample room for development. Construction started in 1841 and the works had 200 employees by the following year ready for repair and maintenance to start in 1843. Swindon Works built the first locomotive for the GWR in 1846. This was the Broad Gauge 2-2-2 *Great Western* and in 1876 the works began building convertible locomotives, then finally discontinuing with Broad Gauge construction in 1891. The first Standard Gauge engine was erected in 1855 and the role continued to 1960 as British Railways Standard Class 9F no. 92220 *Evening Star* was the last steam locomotive built at Swindon. The works had contributed 5,720 locomotives to the railways. At the height of operations, 326 acres were devoted to railway operations at Swindon, with 77 acres under cover. A total staff of 14,000 were engaged on all aspects connected to the railway. In these two images, one of the machine shops is illustrated in the early 20th century.

Opposite and above SWINDON WORKS

The 1860s saw Daniel Gooch join the GWR Board and Joseph Armstrong take over rolling stock matters. At this time there were several new buildings constructed at Swindon, then in the 1870s a major expansion was carried out on land to the west of the original site. A boiler shop, brass foundry, erecting shop, iron foundry, machine shop, paint shop and tender shop comprised the new buildings which came into use during 1874. On the opposite page is the machine shop and the top image is the erecting shop. The latter was replaced by a vast new erecting shop, also built on the west side of the site, in the early 20th century and the original became the boiler shop.

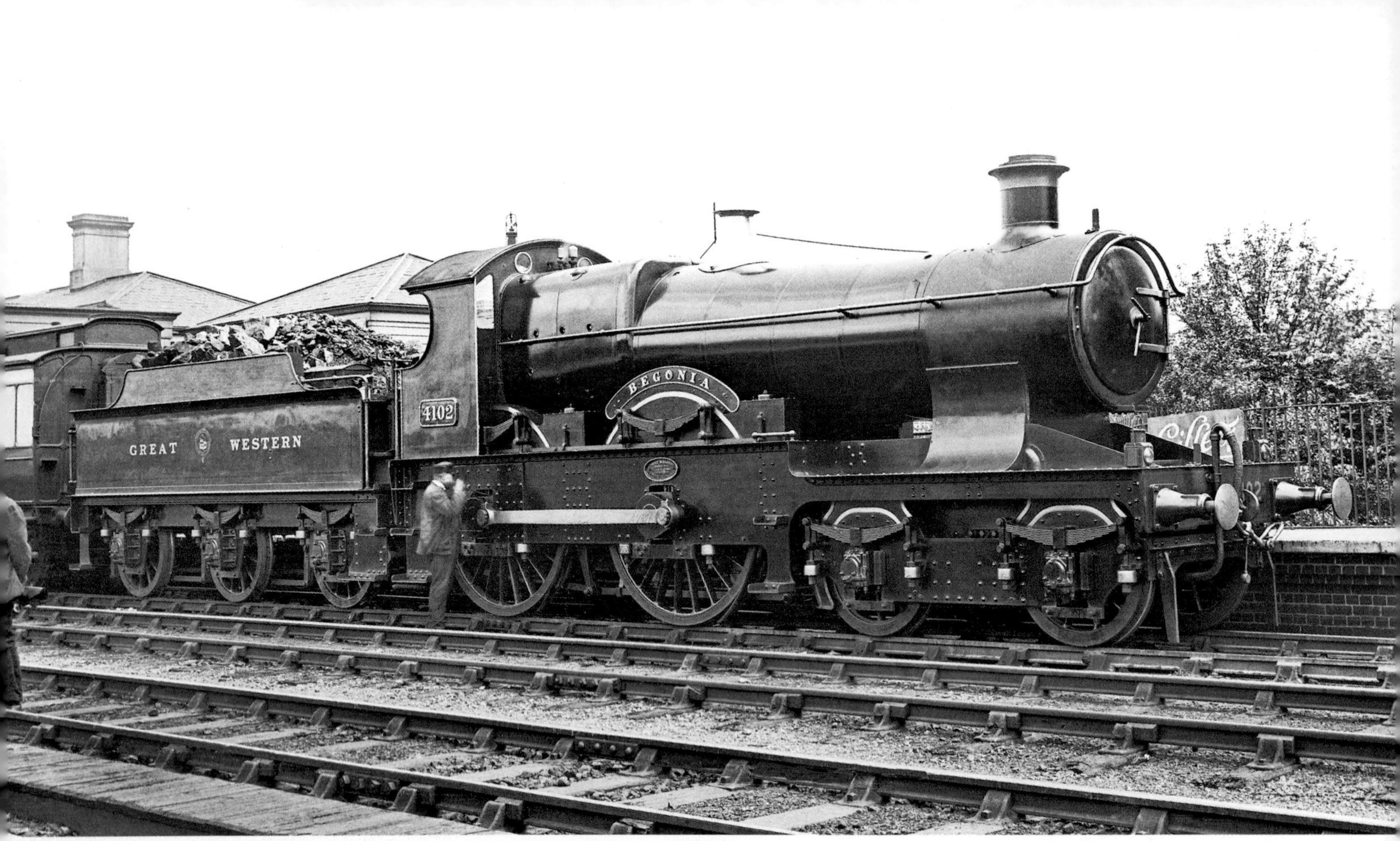
BEGONIA
4102
GREAT WESTERN

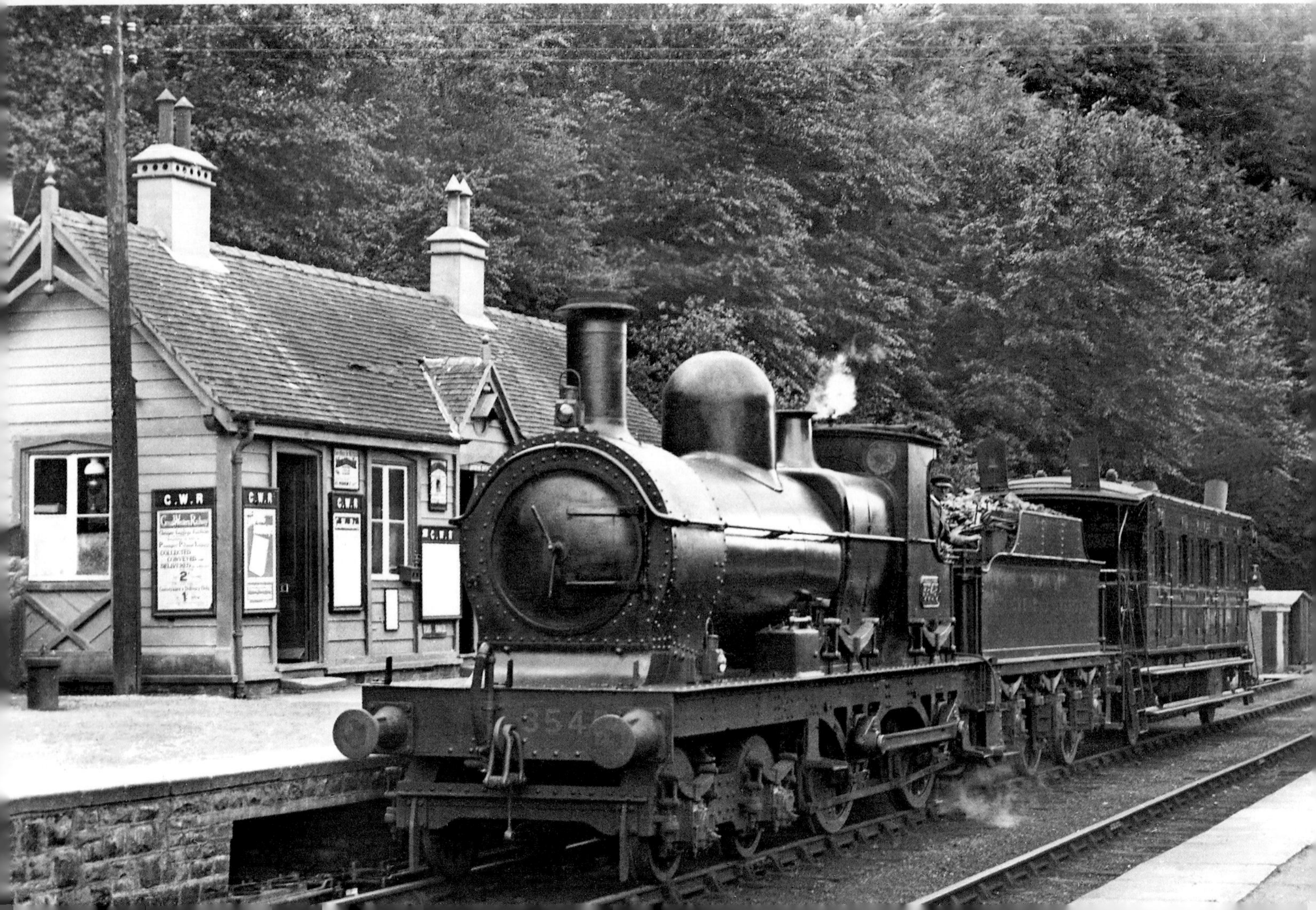
G.W.R
G.W.R
G.W.R
G.W.R
COLLECTED
CONVEYED
DELIVERED

Above **388 CLASS 0-6-0 – NO. 403**
In the mid-1860s, Joseph Armstrong ordered 19 0-6-0 locomotives which formed the basis of the 388 or Standard Goods Class. No. 403 was part of this initial group and in service from February 1867. The locomotive is pictured towards the end shunting at Swindon Works. No. 403 was sent for scrap during March 1921. Photograph courtesy Rail Photoprints.

Opposite above **FLOWER CLASS 4-4-0 – NO. 4102**
Sharing a lineage with the Atbara Class, the Flower Class 4-4-0 was new with several detail differences, such as outside frames and new bogies. Twenty engines were built in 1908. No. 4102 *Begonia* was completed during May and went on to be superheated in January 1911. Originally constructed with slide valves, these were upgraded to piston valves before Grouping. In 1912, the number changed to 4150 and *Begonia* went on to be the last class member in traffic when condemned in May 1931. The locomotive is pictured in 1912 at Oxford. Photograph courtesy Rail Photoprints.

Opposite below **3521 CLASS 4-4-0 – NO. 3545**
No. 3545 started life as a convertible 0-4-2ST, then became an 0-4-4ST Broad Gauge engine, before changing to Standard Gauge. Further work was carried out on the locomotive in August 1900 when made a 4-4-0 tender engine. The boiler at this time was of the round-top parallel type, though changed to a Belpaire firebox in April 1916. No. 3545 is seen after that date, and before withdrawal in April 1931, at Symonds Yat station. This opened on the Ross & Monmouth Railway during 1873 which was operated by the GWR from the beginning. The engine appears to be with a four-wheel inspection saloon. Photograph courtesy Rail Photoprints.

Above **3700 CLASS – NO. 3705**
In the late 19th Century, G.J. Churchward became William Dean's assistant and until the succession he was able to study and plan for the GWR's locomotive requirements in the new century. One of his plans was the replacement of the straight boiler barrel with a tapered cone and the use of a Belpaire firebox. To test the suitability of the Standard No. 4 boiler embodying these features, Atbara Class 4-4-0 no. 3405 *Mauritius* was rebuilt in September 1901. Proving successful, a further nine Atbaras were rebuilt later in the decade and ten new locomotives appeared from Swindon during 1903. No. 3405 became no. 3705 in the 4-4-0 renumbering scheme and was in service to September 1928. The locomotive has been caught near Paddington at a servicing point in 1922. Photograph courtesy Rail Photoprints.

Above **CHURCHWARD 4-6-2 PACIFIC – NO. 111 *THE GREAT BEAR***
A smart gentleman poses with no. 111 *The Great Bear* which is resting inside Old Oak Common shed on 21st May 1921. Built at the same time as the 4000 Class 4-6-0s, the Pacific shared some features with those engines though had a new boiler, wide firebox and one-off tender which utilised bogie wheels. No. 111 was based at Old Oak Common shed from new in February 1908 until withdrawn during January 1924. The locomotive was primarily used between London and Bristol owing to weight restrictions. Photograph from the Norman Preedy Collection courtesy Rail Photoprints.

LOCOMOTIVES – POST GROUPING

Above **4000 CLASS 4-6-0 – NO. 4038**
Following the first two orders for 4000 Class 4-6-0s, were another two orders built from 1909 to 1911. Consisting of ten engines in each, these locomotives were named after Kings and Queens of England. The group was also built new with the standard superheater arrangement. No. 4038 *Queen Berengaria* was completed in January 1911 and is seen here around ten years later passing Twyford East signal box with an express. Photograph by A.L.P. Reavil from Rail Archive Stephenson courtesy Rail-Online.

Opposite above **2221 CLASS 4-4-2T – NO. 2239**
Suburban traffic duties were assigned to Churchward's 2221 Class 4-4-2T upon their introduction to traffic in 1905. A total of 30 were produced up to 1912, with no. 2239 part of the second order for ten engines. Built at Swindon in January 1909, the locomotive was superheated 18 months later and ran up to December 1934. No. 2239 departs Paddington station with a train for Oxford here in 1924. Photograph by F.R. Hebron from Rail Archive Stephenson courtesy Rail-Online.

Opposite below **4073 CLASS 4-6-0 – NO. 5000**
Charles Collett succeeded G.J. Churchward in 1922 and one of his early designs was the 4073 Castle Class 4-6-0. This was an improved version of his predecessor's 4000 Class for use on the main line expresses. The locomotives were an immediate success and the London Midland & Scottish Railway was intrigued, owing to the company's own stock not performing particularly well at the time. A loan of a Castle was negotiated in 1926 and no. 5000 *Launceston Castle* went to the West Coast Main Line for trials lasting a month. The LMSR was impressed and responded with the three-cylinder Royal Scot Class 4-6-0. In this image, the staff at Euston has gathered to inspect no. 5000. Photograph from Rail Archive Stephenson courtesy Rail-Online.

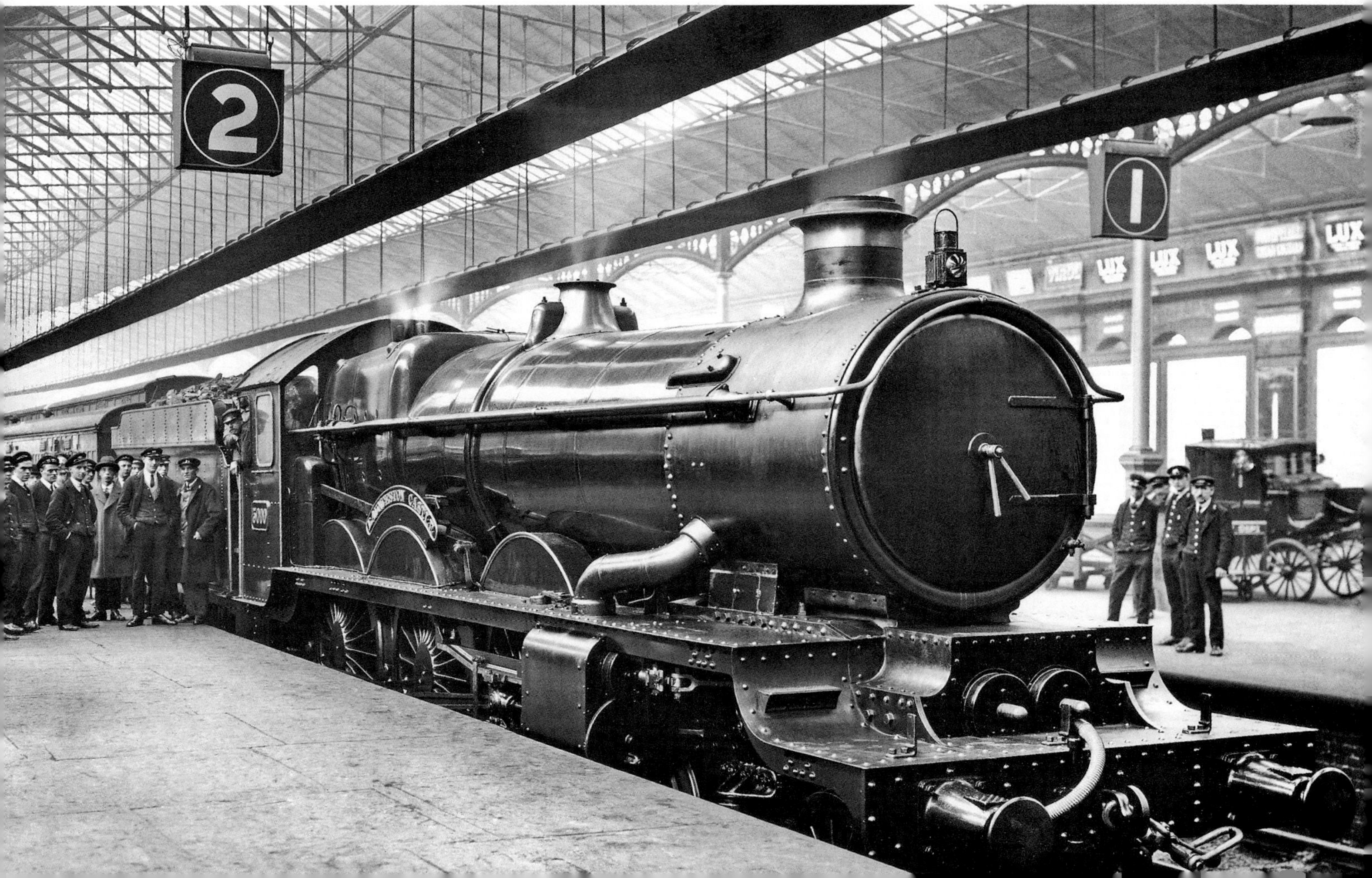

Opposite and above **SWINDON WORKS**

Small-scale additions and alterations were carried out at Swindon to the end of the 19th century. As the 1900s started, Churchward was ready to take over and the workshops were in need of expansion. Again on the west side of the site, a 480 ft by 485 ft steel-framed erecting shop was installed in the first years of the 20th century. There were 20 repair bays either side of a central aisle served by a traverser. Following the First World War, though authorised before, an extension of a similar design was constructed adding another 60 bays to the workshop capacity. The opening of the first erecting shop relieved the pressure on the original site and the old erecting shop was made the boiler shop. The scene opposite was captured in the latter during the early 20th century, whilst that above shows the new erecting shop. Visible under repair is a Churchward 4200 Class 2-8-0T no. 5223, Churchward 3700 Class 4-4-0 no. 3715 *City of Hereford* and suspended in the air to the rear is 4000 Class 4-6-0 no. 4034 *Queen Adelaide*. The first erecting shop had two 50-ton capacity overhead cranes whilst the new erecting shop possessed 100-ton capacity examples.

Above **SOUTH DEVON RAILWAY 2-4-0T – NO. 1299**
Absorbed by the GWR in 1876, the South Devon Railway passed over 85 Broad Gauge locomotives. Three other engines were under construction at the time and these were taken to Swindon for completion. They took the form of Standard Gauge 2-4-0T locomotives. Originally to be named *Jupiter*, this engine had to settle for no. 1299 when placed in service from December 1878. During April 1881 the engine was converted to carry a crane and for several years subsequently found employment in the Reading area. Latterly, no. 1299 was a works shunter at Swindon and is seen there c. 1928. The engine was condemned during September 1936. Photograph courtesy Rail Photoprints.

Opposite above **6000 CLASS 4-6-0 – NO. 6004**
When Charles Collett took over as Chief Mechanical Engineer he was limited in his designs owing to permanent way restrictions. As the infrastructure was improved during the 1920s, he was able to produce a new version of his 4073 Class 4-6-0. This had a modified boiler, altered piston stroke and smaller driving wheels to meet a stipulated tractive effort approaching 40,000 lb. Between 1927 and 1930 Swindon built 30 6000 or King Class 4-6-0s. No. 6004 *King George III* was part of the first batch and completed during July 1927. The engine is pictured travelling towards the summit of Dainton bank a relatively short time later in 1929. The class remained the premier engines on the GWR to 1962. Photograph by Robert Brookman from Rail Archive Stephenson courtesy Rail-Online.

Opposite below **2361 CLASS 0-6-0 – NO. 2370**
At the turn of the century, the GWR wanted a better connection to the Midlands via Bicester and Princes Risborough. This project was entered into with the Great Central Railway, with the latter company spurring eastward to Marylebone station at Northolt Junction. Dean 2361 Class 0-6-0 no. 2370 has a northbound goods train at this point in 1930. Constructed in December 1885, the locomotive was in traffic to March 1935. Photograph by George R. Grigs from Rail Archive Stephenson courtesy Rail-Online.

Above 3700 CLASS 4-4-0 – NO. 3718

One of the new build 3700 Class 4-4-0s, no. 3718 *City of Winchester*, is at Newbury station with a train of empty milk wagons, c. 1925. For many years the product was moved in churns loaded into dedicated wagons like these, yet around 1930, the introduction of milk tankers allowed many thousands of gallons to be transported around the country. Mainly with 3,000-gallon capacity, a wagon could serve milk to 30,000 people. The GWR had much of the British milk traffic and moved a good deal of the 300 million gallons produced annually in the 1930s. No. 3718 was withdrawn in October 1927. Photograph by C.R. Gordon Stuart from Rail Archive Stephenson courtesy Rail-Online.

Opposite above 517 CLASS 0-4-2T – NO. 1440

No. 1440 was built around halfway in the construction period of George Armstrong's 517 Class 0-4-2T. New in December 1877, the locomotive's career lasted to September 1935 and was possible owing to several upgrades in design and boiler over these years. In the early 1930s, a number of 517 Class members were fitted for auto-train working, including no. 1440 which has a branch service at Abbotsbury station. The latter was at the end of the Abbotsbury branch that left the line to Weymouth just north of the town. Opened in 1885, the branch survived to the end of 1952 when closed completely. Photograph courtesy Rail-Online.

Opposite below 2301 CLASS 0-6-0 – NO. 2358

The Newtown & Machynlleth Railway built a three-road shed for servicing locomotives working the line at Machynlleth in 1863. A second building was provided as an extension to the original during the late 19th century when the line was part of the Cambrian Railways. Both were located at the eastern end of the station south of the running lines and were used until the closure to steam in December 1966. Dean 2301 Class 0-6-0 no. 2358 is on the turntable there c. 1930. New from Swindon during December 1884, the engine was condemned in November 1934. Photograph from Rail Archive Stephenson courtesy Rail-Online.

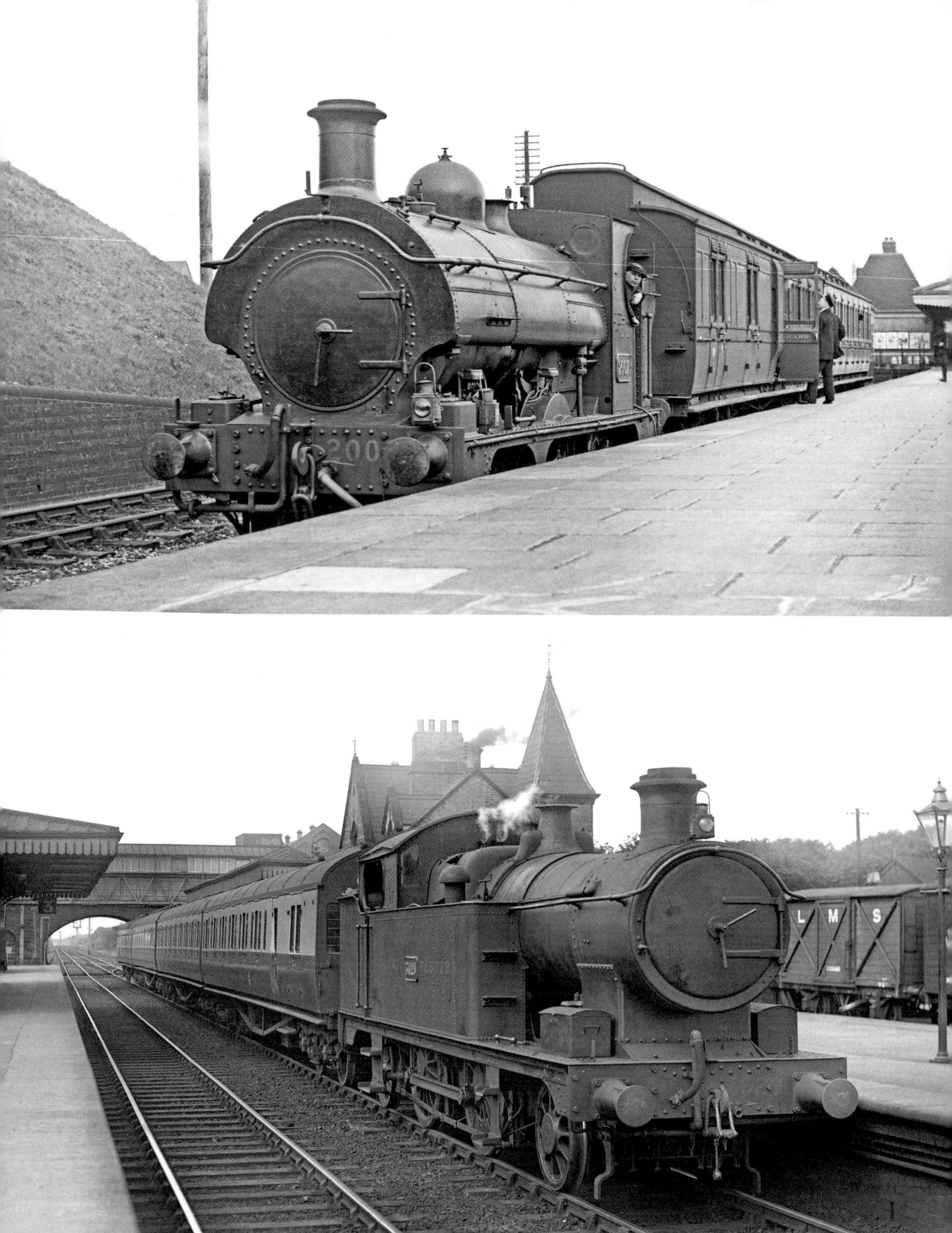

Above **6000 CLASS 4-6-0 – NO. 6008**
An express service stands against the platform at Paddington station with 6000 Class no. 6008 *King James II* in the 1930s. The locomotive was new to Plymouth Laira in March 1928, though soon after moved to Wolverhampton and the shed held the allocation to the 1950s. Photograph from the David P. Williams Archive courtesy Rail-Online.

Opposite above **1901 CLASS 0-6-0ST – NO. 2007**
From Newbury on the Reading to Taunton line, a branch ran for 12 miles to reach Lambourn. Opened in 1898, the line was active for passengers until 1960, whilst freight persisted to 1973. 1901 Class 0-6-0ST no. 2007 waits to depart from Newbury station with a branch train c. 1935. Photograph from Rail Archive Stephenson courtesy Rail-Online.

Opposite below **3600 CLASS 2-4-2T – NO. 3629**
The GWR attempted to introduce a 4-4-0T at the turn of the century but this was a failure and the company turned to the 2-4-0T type used previously. Yet the wheel arrangement was modified to become a 2-4-2T which proved acceptable. In three years from 1900, 31 3600 Class locomotives were erected at Swindon. No. 3629 was the penultimate engine completed in December 1903. The class was used on suburban services and no. 3629 has a Birkenhead to Helsby train here at Hooton station, c. 1930. The locomotive was withdrawn in November 1931. Photograph by H. Gordon Tidey from Rail Archive Stephenson courtesy Rail-Online.

Above 3521 CLASS 4-4-0 – NO. 3559
No. 3559 was the last of the 0-4-2ST Broad Gauge engines built in 1889, though was soon after made an 0-4-4ST. During January 1901, the locomotive became a 4-4-0 with a large taper boiler. Superheating was only carried out shortly after Grouping and no. 3559 was the last class member in traffic when condemned during November 1931. At this time the engine was at Worcester. In the period before withdrawal, the locomotive has been caught arriving at Southampton with a train from Cheltenham. Photograph by B. Whicher from Rail Archive Stephenson courtesy Rail-Online.

Opposite above 3800 CLASS 4-4-2T – NO. 3818
Kensal Green gas works sat beside the GWR main line to Paddington from 1845 to 1970 when decommissioned, though the gasholder framework remained on site until recently. Churchward 3800 Class 4-4-0 no. 3818 *County of Radnor* passes by with a train in August 1931. Photograph by George R. Grigs from Rail Archive Stephenson courtesy Rail-Online.

Opposite below 6000 CLASS 4-6-0 – NO. 6008
A clerestory carriage leads the formation of the 14.10 express between Paddington and Birkenhead hauled by 6000 Class no. 6008 *King James II*. Seen in July 1931, the engine had recently left Plymouth for Wolverhampton. Photograph by George R. Grigs from Rail Archive Stephenson courtesy Rail-Online.

Above **2221 CLASS 4-4-2T – NO. 2224**
First-batch 2221 Class locomotive no. 2224 passes Kensal Green with a suburban train consisting of clerestory carriages on 7th August 1932. The locomotive had just a year left before withdrawal, ending a career lasting just under 30 years. Photograph by James R. Clark from Rail Archive Stephenson courtesy Rail-Online.

Opposite above **517 CLASS 0-4-2T – NO. 1428**
Dauntsey station was a late addition to the London to Bristol line, opening in February 1868. Almost ten years later, the station became a junction when the branch to Malmesbury was built. In the late 19th century, the GWR received authorisation to construct a line of 30 miles from Wootton Bassett to Stoke Gifford which reduced the length of the existing route and removed difficult features of that section. Completed in 1903, this cut through the Malmesbury branch and eventually the Dauntsey connection was seen as wasteful and changed to the new line at Little Somerford. This occurred in 1933 and the branch remained active to passengers until 1951. In June 1932, 517 Class 0-4-2T no. 1428 is seen at Dauntsey station with a branch service. Dauntsey station closed in 1965. Photograph by George R. Grigs from Rail Archive Stephenson courtesy Rail-Online.

Opposite below **3800 CLASS 4-4-0 – NO. 3827**
A westbound train of milk empties approaches West Drayton & Yiewsley station, 13 miles from Paddington, behind 3800 Class no. 3827 *County of Gloucester* during June 1931. West Drayton station was new with the main line in 1838 but was later resited and renamed before the end of the century. Since 1974, the station reverted to the original name. No. 3827 had just six months left in traffic. Photograph by George R. Grigs from Rail Archive Stephenson courtesy Rail-Online.

© H. Gordon Tidey/Rail Archive Stephenson

Above **2361 CLASS 0-6-0 – NO. 2373**
Part of William Dean's abandoned standard design series, the 2361 Class 0-6-0 was a group of 20 locomotives built at Swindon Works during the mid-1880s. Despite their small number, the class managed to deliver around 50 years of service. No. 2373 was new in February 1886 and active to November 1934. A short time before this date, the engine is engaged on a pick-up goods train which has reached Ruislip and Ickenham station. This was located on the GW & GC Joint Line just a short distance from Northolt Junction. Later rebuilt by British Railways for use by the underground, the station's name was changed to West Ruislip. Photograph by C.R.L. Coles from Rail Archive Stephenson courtesy Rail-Online.

Opposite above **4900 CLASS 4-6-0 – NO. 4906**
Using Churchward 2-6-0s on mixed traffic duties, the GWR found that by the mid-1920s these engines were struggling in the face of increased loads. Collett decided to modify a 2900 Class 4-6-0 with upgraded features and this engine was tested extensively before the design for the new 4900 or Hall Class 4-6-0 was finalised. A stream of engines flowed from Swindon between 1928 to 1943 when 258 were in service. No. 4906 *Bradfield Hall* was an early example, completed in January 1929. The engine is at Torquay station with a train for Kingswear in the early 1930s. Photograph by H. Gordon Tidey from Rail Archive Stephenson courtesy Rail-Online.

Opposite below **3252 CLASS 4-4-0 – NO. 3256**
Travelling along the through line at Oxford station on 10th June 1933 is 3252 Class no. 3256 *Guinevere*. The locomotive had been in traffic from August 1895, though had originally carried no. 3257. Just before the Second World War, the engine was taken out of traffic and nominally rebuilt as a 3200 Class 4-4-0. No. 3256 was reborn as no. 3228, but was not named, in November 1939 and was the last transformation carried out. Photograph by Les Hanson from the David Hanson Archive courtesy Rail-Online.

Above **2021 CLASS 0-6-0PT – NO. 2141**
In Swindon Works on 2nd June 1935 is Dean 2021 Class 0-6-0PT no. 2141. The locomotive started life as an 0-6-0ST in March 1904, built at Wolverhampton Works, and has just undergone the transformation to an 0-6-0PT. Though these conversions had started in 1912, the process continued to Nationalisation. The locomotive ran for another 15 years until condemned during October 1950. Photograph by Les Hanson from the David Hanson Archive courtesy Rail-Online.

Opposite above **2900 CLASS 4-6-0 – NO. 2931**
Testing the performance of steam locomotives was carried out via instruments fitted to the engine or latterly trailing behind in the form of a dedicated carriage. The testing was done from the earliest days of the railways but had disadvantages. Not until the end of the 19th century was a testing plant developed and this was located in America. Churchward was perhaps inspired by this development, as part of the workshops' modernisations of the early 20th century included the provision of a testing station. Initially limited to 500 horsepower, an upgrade was carried out in the mid-1930s and the plant had a capacity of 2,000 horsepower. Sir Nigel Gresley of the London & North Eastern Railway was a vocal promoter of a national facility which was eventually built post-war and operated under British Railways. Yet, Swindon remained active and accepted a number of classes to the end of steam. Here, on 2nd June 1935, 2900 Class 4-6-0 no. 2931 *Arlington Court* has been placed on the apparatus to demonstrate the operation for a works open day. Photograph by Les Hanson from the David Hanson Archive courtesy Rail-Online.

Opposite below **DIESEL RAILCAR – NO. 13**
With the rise of the internal combustion engine in the early 20th century, railway companies began to experiment with the technology. The GWR acquired a petrol-electric railcar in 1911 which was not particularly successful owing to engine problems and withdrawal occurred after the First World War. The next foray took place in the early 1930s using a diesel engine and a streamlined body. This prototype was successful and another 37 were built up to 1942. No. 13 was constructed by the Gloucester Railway Carriage & Wagon Company in 1936. The unit was quite new when pictured here at Carmarthen station on 13th August 1936. Photograph by Les Hanson from the David Hanson Archive courtesy Rail-Online.

Above **2800 CLASS 2-8-0 – NO. 2817**
Just as Churchward introduced the 4-6-2 Pacific wheel arrangement to Britain, so was the 2-8-0, which likely originated in America. In 1903 he produced a prototype, no. 97, and this was tested extensively to determine the final specifications. This saw the design change to a taper boiler with increased pressure, larger cylinders and larger valves. Production commenced in 1905 with a batch of 20 locomotives and amongst this number was no. 2817 which was ready by December. Some 22 years after this date, the engine has been caught at Banbury with an iron ore train for Guest, Keen & Baldwins steel works, South Wales. No. 2817 was in traffic until March 1959. Photograph by G.R. Grigs from Rail Archive Stephenson courtesy Rail-Online.

Opposite above **6800 CLASS 4-6-0 – NO. 6824**
The Churchward 4300 Class 2-6-0 was deemed life-expired in the early 1930s leading to their withdrawal. In their place, Collett produced the 6800 Class 4-6-0 which utilised some of the components from the 4300 Class. A total of 80 were built at Swindon between 1936 and 1939. No. 6824 *Ashley Grange* was a product of the works in January 1937 and is seen under construction there during December 1936. The locomotive went on to work in South Wales, the South West and Midlands up to withdrawal in April 1964. Photograph from Rail Archive Stephenson courtesy Rail-Online.

Opposite below **DIESEL RAILCAR – NO. 11**
The first four streamlined diesel railcars were built by Park Royal, then the next 13 appeared from the Gloucester Railway Carriage & Wagon Company. The remainder were the product of Swindon Works. No. 11 was manufactured by the Gloucester Railway Carriage & Wagon Company during 1936 and a feature of this, and no. 10 and no. 12 also in the batch, was the inclusion of a lavatory. The unit is seen to the north of Limpley Stoke with Dundas Aqueduct in the background on 15th May 1936. Photograph from Rail Archive Stephenson courtesy Rail Photoprints.

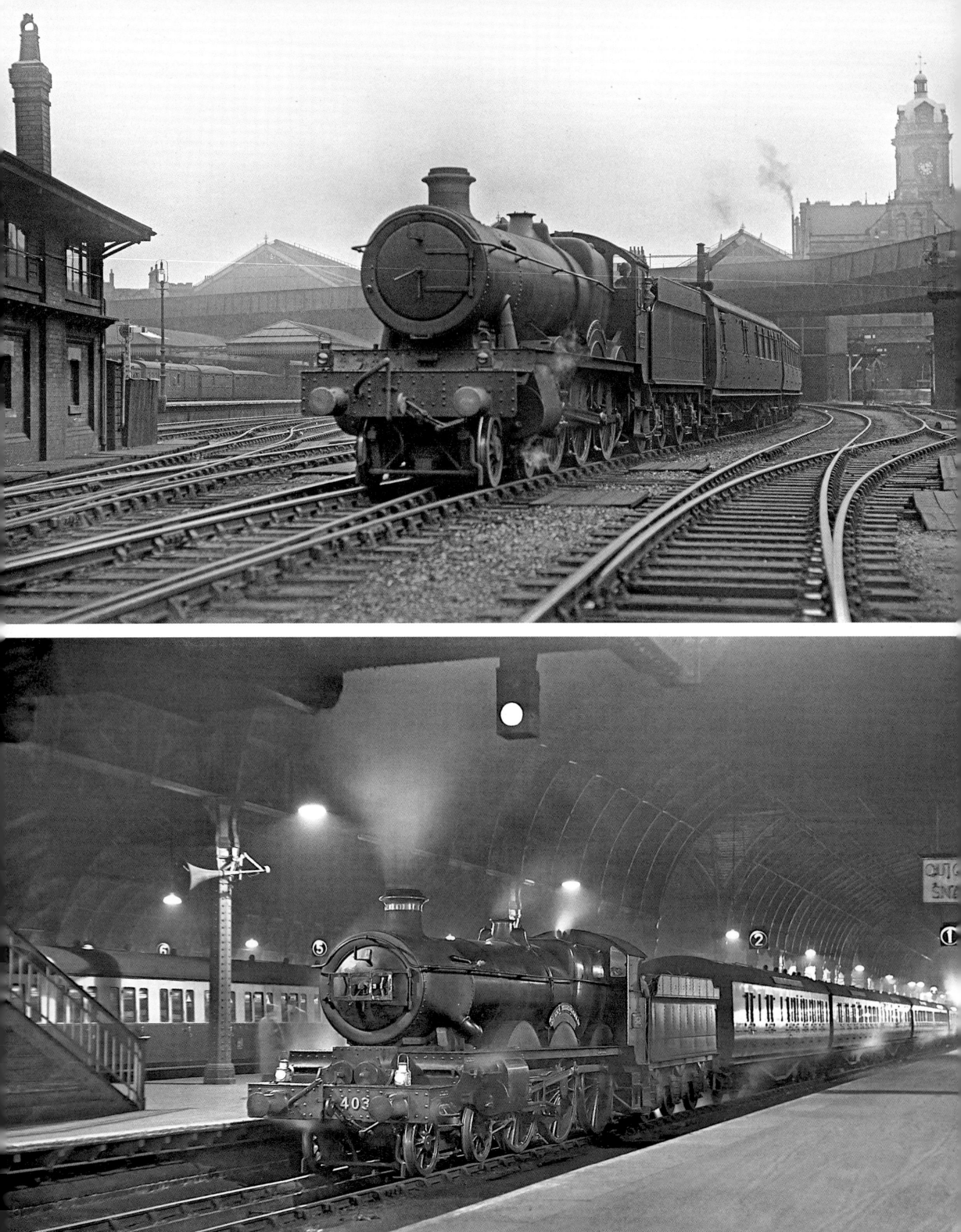

Above **4073 CLASS 4-6-0 – NO. 5043**
In the mid-1930s, the 3200 Class rebuilds were set to carry names of Earls associated with the GWR. Yet, these were soon after transferred to existing 4073 Castle Class locomotives. No. 5043 *Barbury Castle* was completed at Swindon in March 1936 and ran for around 18 months before rechristened *Earl of Mount Edgcumbe*. The engine has been pictured at Rushcombe with the 17.30 Paddington to Plymouth express during 1937/1938. When withdrawn in 1963, no. 5043 was dispatched to Woodham Brothers scrapyard and later rescued by the Birmingham Railway Museum in the early 1970s. The locomotive was the subject of a restoration project in the 1990s/2000s. A total of eight 4073 Class engines were saved and no. 5043 is one of two in steam at present. Photograph by C.R.L. Coles from Rail Archive Stephenson courtesy Rail-Online.

Opposite above **4900 CLASS 4-6-0 – NO. 5973**
An excursion has brought Southern Railway carriage stock northward from Bournemouth to Nottingham Victoria on 30th May 1937. The locomotive is 4900 Class no. 5973 *Rolleston Hall*. With the opening of the GC & GW Joint Line, the GCR began offering cross-country services and GWR locomotives worked as far as Nottingham. No. 5973 was only a month old when pictured and was in service to September 1962. Photograph by T.G. Hepburn from Rail Archive Stephenson courtesy Rail-Online.

Opposite below **4000 CLASS 4-6-0 – NO. 4038**
4000 Class no. 4038 *Queen Berengaria* has been caught in a nighttime pose at Paddington station on 19th April 1938. Whilst a no. 3 superheater had first appeared in the previous batch of ten 4000 Class engines, from no. 4031 this became standard and included no. 4038 when built in January 1911. The locomotive was condemned at Westbury shed during April 1952. Photograph by Les Hanson from the David Hanson Archive courtesy Rail-Online.

Above **4900 CLASS 4-6-0 – NO. 5960**
On 6th February 1939, 4900 Class no. 5960 *Saint Edmund Hall* approaches the platform at Swindon station with an express for Bristol. The locomotive had just celebrated three years in traffic and was active to September 1962. Under BR, no. 5960 was mainly employed at Oxford. Photograph by George C. Lander courtesy Rail Photoprints.

Opposite above **3200 CLASS 4-4-0 – NO. 3265**
Seen in the late 1930s, 3200 Class no. 3265 *Tre Pol and Pen* has a stopping train from Whitchurch to Oswestry at Abermule station. The latter was opened by the Oswestry & Newton Railway in the early 1860s though the company was soon absorbed by the Cambrian Railways. No. 3265 was in service to December 1949. Photograph from Rail Archive Stephenson courtesy Rail-Online.

Opposite below **5205 CLASS 2-8-0T – NO. 5211**
In 1910 Churchward built the 4200 Class 2-8-0T for heavy coal trains running on the lines in South Wales which had difficult gradients. To further cater for the work, Collett slightly modified the design and the 5205 Class was introduced during 1923. No. 5211 was amongst the first batch of ten and a further 90 followed up to 1940. The locomotive stands in the shed yard at Landore on 28th May 1939. Also present are two 4000 Class 4-6-0s, no. 4003 *Lode Star* and no. 4050 *Princess Alice*. No. 5211 was condemned at Aberdare in May 1964. Photograph from the J. Lander Collection courtesy Rail Photoprints.

Above **6000 CLASS 4-6-0 – NO. 6014**

Railway engineers were always examining ways to improve the efficiency of the steam locomotive. In the 1920s and 1930s, when there was a decline in revenues and financial pressures, an interest was raised in streamlining which reduced the air resistance to provide a saving in fuel consumption. Some applications were exercises in design, whilst others were specifically produced using wind tunnel tests. In Britain, all four railway companies developed some form of streamlining. The GWR's version was applied to 6000 Class no. 6014 *King Henry VII* in March 1935, pre-dating Sir Nigel Gresley's A4 Pacific Class by two months. No. 6014 has been caught at Old Oak Common shed later in the year during September and would go on to run in the form until returned to stock in 1943. Photograph courtesy Rail Photoprints.

Opposite above **4000 CLASS 4-6-0 – NO. 4021**

An engineman gives a friendly wave as 4000 Class no. 4021 *The British Monarch* leaves Nottingham Victoria station with empty stock for Basford Carriage Sidings on 30th May 1939. The locomotive was completed in June 1909 as *King Edward*, yet with the introduction of the 6000 King Class, the names were redeployed. No. 4021 was initially *British Monarch* but from late 1927 was *The British Monarch*. The engine survived to October 1952. Photograph by J.P. Wilson from Rail Archive Stephenson courtesy Rail-Online.

Opposite below **4900 CLASS 4-6-0 – NO. 4974**

By the early 20th century, the GWR had outgrown stabling facilities at Westbourne Park and a new site was found at Acton, known as Old Oak Common. When opened in 1906, four roundhouses were under one roof and an extensive repair shop was provided. This view inside the building was taken just before Nationalisation and features 4900 Class no. 4974 *Talgarth Hall* amongst several other unidentified engines. The Hall was new in January 1930 and active to April 1962. Around the latter date, work to convert Old Oak Common shed to diesel servicing was underway and the new depot was ready in 1965. Photograph by C.R.L. Coles from Rail Archive Stephenson courtesy Rail-Online.

CARRIAGES

Above **BROAD GAUGE CARRIAGES**
A sea of Broad Gauge coaches is seen at Swindon following the conversion to Standard Gauge during May 1892. Over 400 would go on to be rebuilt, whilst around 100 had to be scrapped. One of the reasons Brunel favoured the Broad Gauge was this allowed the use of 4 ft diameter wheels which reduced axlebox problems.

Opposite above **THIRD-CLASS CARRIAGE**
The early GWR coaches drew from stagecoach design and three classes were offered to passengers. Initially the company purchased stock from the trade, then established a carriage works at Swindon in 1860. During 1848, the GWR introduced all-iron third-class carriages which was an innovative departure from the wooden carriages built before. This was also an improvement for third class as the GWR originally offered open accommodation for those passengers. The type was in service to the 1860s/1870s.

Opposite below **FIRST-CLASS CARRIAGE**
Dating from 1850, this first-class carriage had three compartments carried on four wheels. Made by Messrs Wright, Birmingham, the firm surprisingly utilised papier mâché for the body sides. The material was evidently successful as another ten years or so passed before the GWR moved on to other forms.

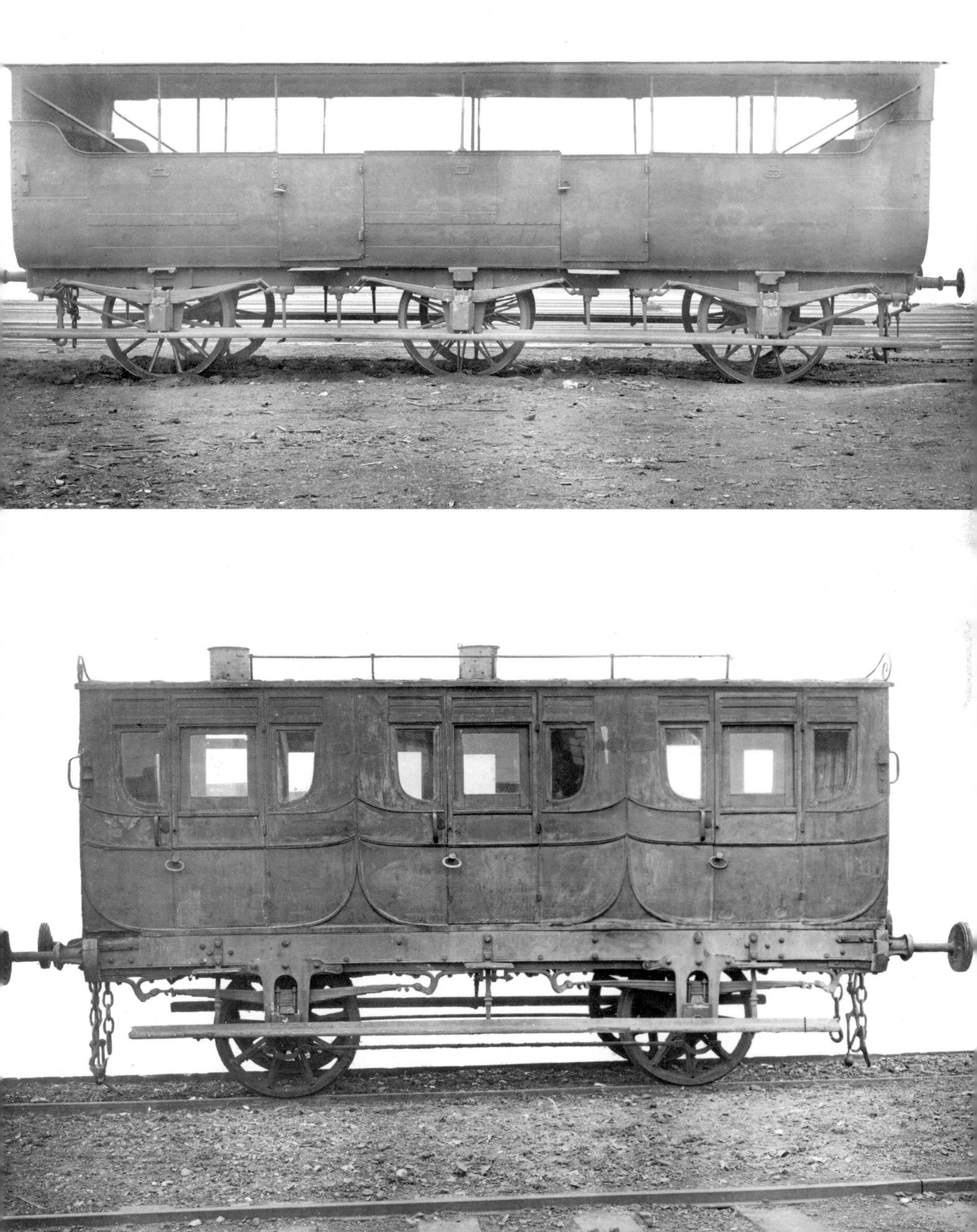

Above **ROYAL TRAIN**
The GWR constructed a Broad Gauge carriage for Queen Victoria in the late 1840s. This was used for the Royal Train for many years, being converted to Standard Gauge and upgraded several times. A new saloon appeared in 1874 and the two carriages were used when required with others. The Royal Train has been recoded here in the late 19th century, with Joseph Armstrong Queen Class 2-2-2 no. 55 *Queen* leading followed by a brake van, first-class saloon, saloon, Queen's saloon (1874), Queen's carriage (1848), first saloon, saloon, saloon, van.

Opposite above **FIRST-CLASS SALOON CARRIAGE**
This first-class saloon began life as a first-class sleeping carriage. Built in 1881, the coach originally had six berths and two lavatories.

Opposite middle **TRAVELLING POST OFFICE**
The 11th November 1830 marked the first time mail was moved by locomotive. This was on the Liverpool & Manchester Railway and by the end of the decade all companies were compelled to transport the post on their lines. At the same time, a carriage for sorting mail was developed. The GWR ran the first mail-only train from London to Bristol during 1855 and at the end of the decade, the company developed an existing idea for the transfer of post between carriage and a suitable receptacle lineside whilst in movement. By the early 20th century, approx. 130 travelling post offices were active on British railways. One of these was no. 653 which was built in 1888 and pictured around the 1920s.

Opposite below **THIRD-CLASS CARRIAGE**
The Monmouth Railway & Canal Co. connected the coalfield and steel works at Newport in the late 1700s and in the mid-1800s upgraded the system to the standard of the time. Independent to 1875, the GWR took over the company. The MR&CCo. operated their own stock, including this third-class four-wheel carriage built by Messrs Wright & Sons Ltd c. 1860. The vehicle is seen after being taken into GWR stock.

Above **QUEEN'S SALOON**
The Queen's saloon was made in 1850 and rebuilt at Swindon during 1874. Supported by two fixed bogies, the body was over 30 ft long containing a saloon, compartment and lavatory. The circular disc on the top left allowed the Royal traveller to communicate with the enginemen. In 1903 the carriage was replaced following several upgrades over the years.

Above **GWR FIRST CORRIDOR TRAIN**
Headed by Dean 3001 Class 2-2-2, the GWR's first corridor train has been pictured in the early 1890s. Apart from the leading brake van, all are clerestory eight-wheel vehicles. The capacity of the train was 210 passengers: 34 first class; 48 second class; 128 third class.

Opposite below **ROYAL SALOON**
In 1874, Queen Victoria received a new saloon built to the Standard Gauge as most journeys were occurring on those lines. The vehicle was similar to the predecessor at the behest of Her Majesty, featuring a central saloon which was larger than typical giving rise to the bulge in the roof. There were also compartments and toilets at each end. For the Queen's Diamond Jubilee, the GWR planned to replace the saloon, yet she commanded that the compartment remained unaltered and this section was incorporated into a new carriage. This survived to 1912 and served in the funerals of both Queen Victoria and Edward VII.

Below **COMPOSITE CORRIDOR CARRIAGE**
A composite second/third-class carriage, no. 1602, built to diagram R.122.

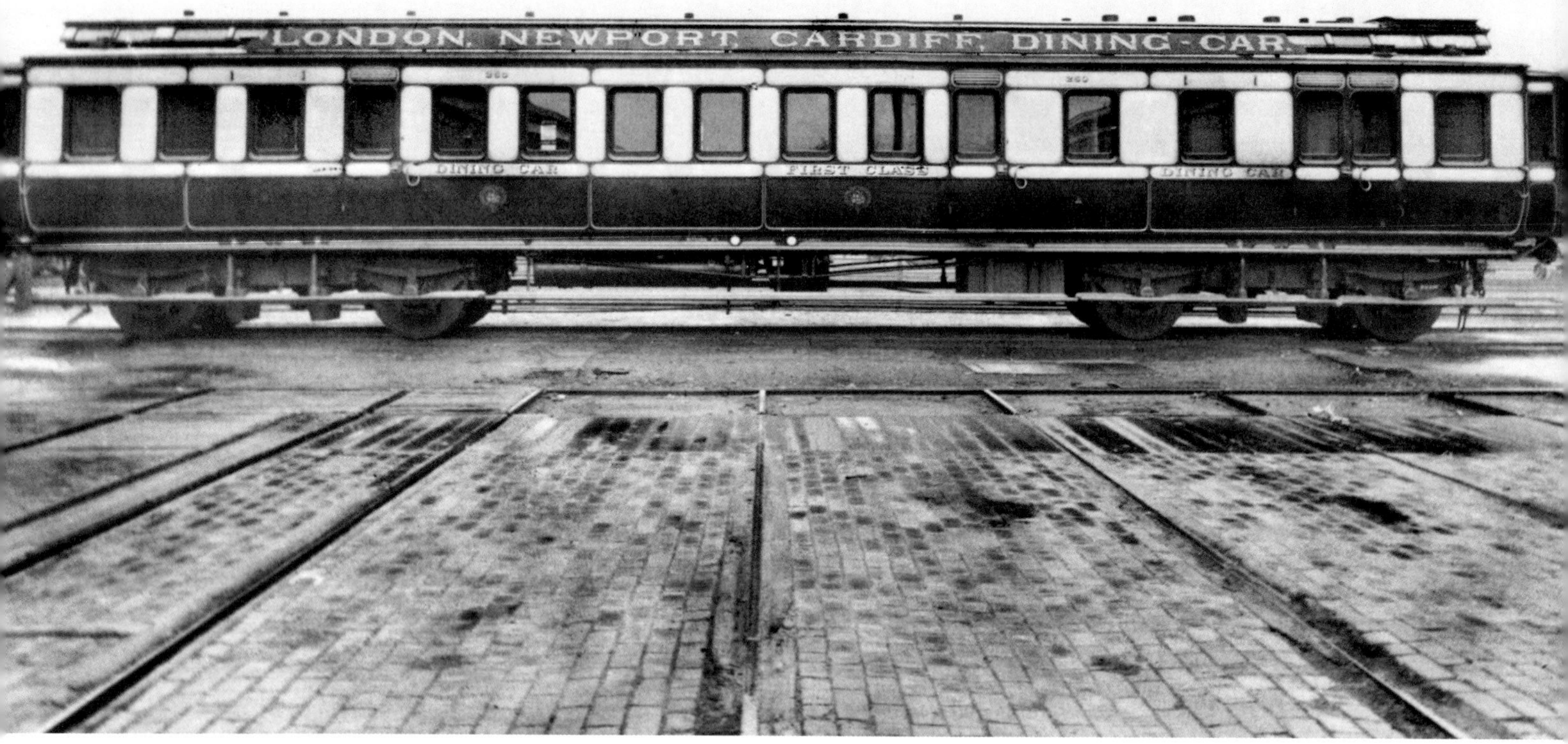
LONDON, NEWPORT, CARDIFF, DINING-CAR.
DINING CAR
FIRST CLASS
DINING CAR

G W R
REFRESHMENT CAR

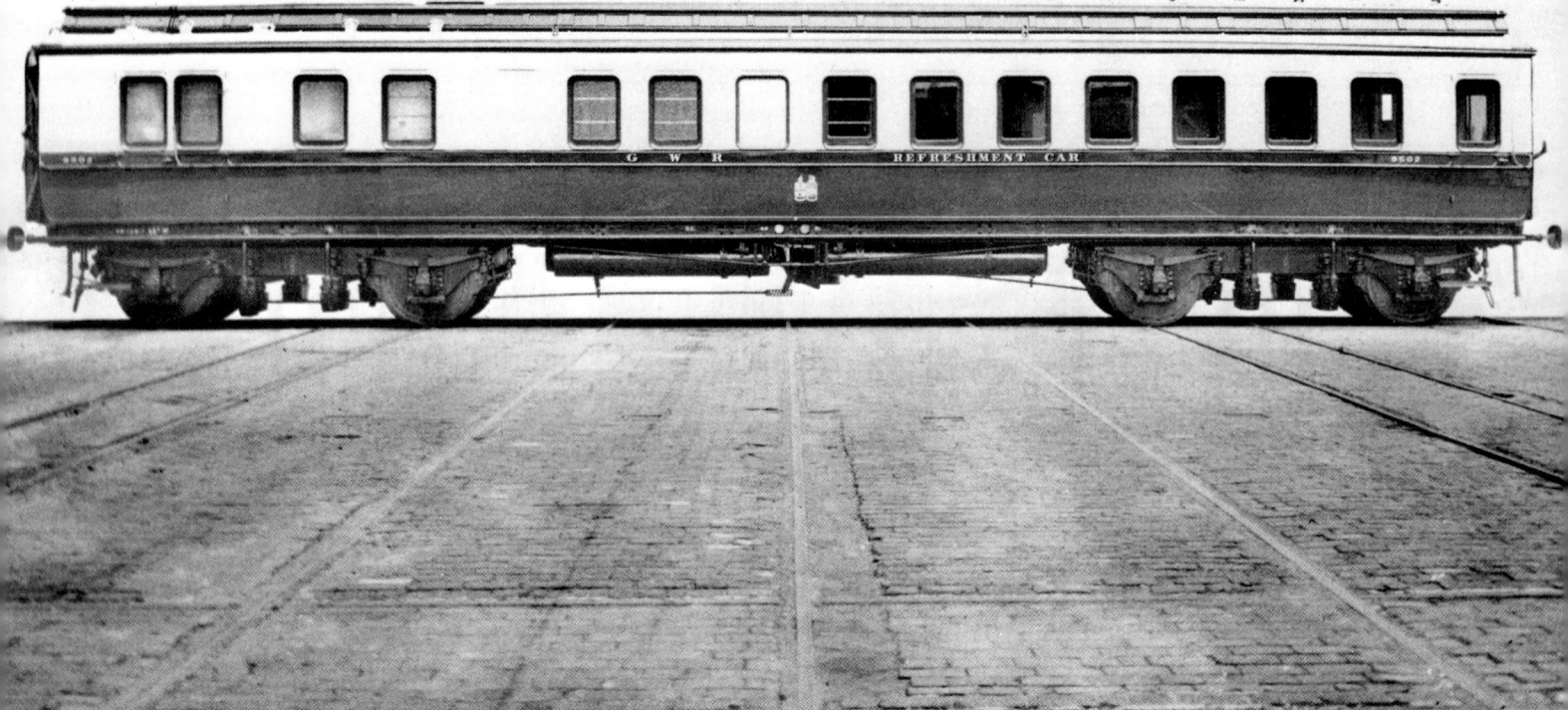

Above **ROYAL TRAIN 1897**
As mentioned, 1897 was the year of the Diamond Jubilee of Queen Victoria and the GWR marked the occasion by constructing five new carriages so the Royal suite could travel between London and Windsor in renewed grandeur. Costing £40,000, the set consisted of two brake vans, two saloons (nos 233 and 224) and first-class carriage (no. 283), along with the rebuilt Royal saloon. The full train has been assembled here for a period portrait.

Opposite above **COMPOSITE DINING CARRIAGE**
A composite dining carriage, no. 250, from 1896 (diagram H2) has South Wales destination boards installed in this image. Seating was for 16 in first class and 18 in second class, with a division existing between the two in the form of sliding doors. The total length of the carriage was 56 ft.

Opposite below **REFRESHMENT CARRIAGE**
The same carriage from the photograph opposite above has received a change of livery, number (9502) and branding, becoming known as a refreshment car. When built, the vehicle was amongst the first batch of dining cars built for the GWR.

Above and opposite DREADNOUGHT STOCK

Churchward had an affinity for American railways and was inspired by practices in the country. As a result in the early 20th century he made a drastic change with the carriage stock by enlarging them considerably from 56 ft to 68 ft and as wide and tall as the loading gauge would allow. These Dreadnought coaches also dispensed with the clerestory roof. The main benefit of the design change was increased capacity, with around a third more people being accommodated. The longer body also necessitated the design of the underframe to be improved. The interiors of two Dreadnought dining cars of the period are seen here.

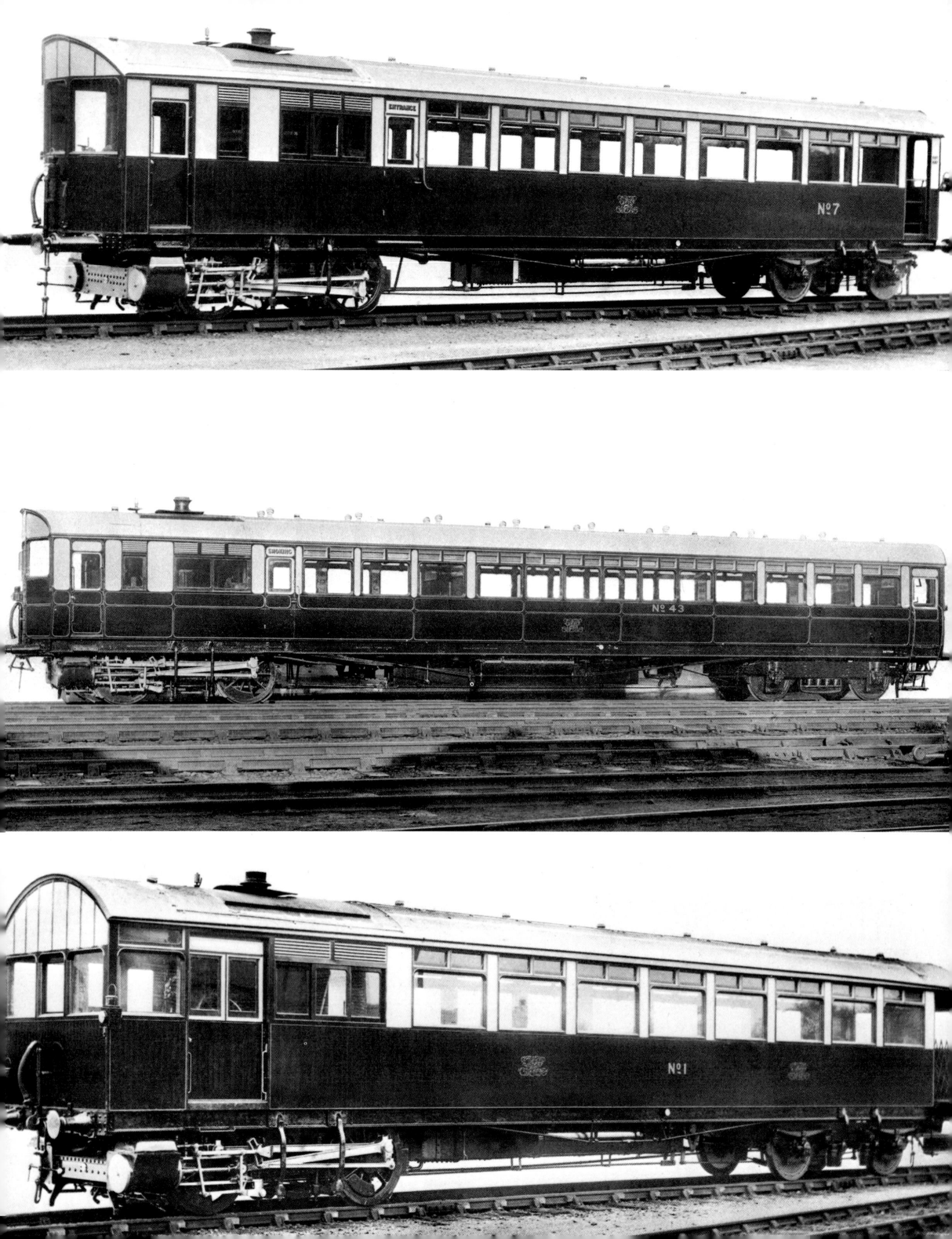

Above **STEAM RAIL MOTOR – NO. 15**
Though the majority of the steam rail motors were built at Swindon, some contractors contributed. Two, nos 15 and 16 were purchased from Kerr, Stuart & Co. and delivered during November 1905. The pair soon failed to measure up to the Swindon product and no. 15 was sold to the Nidd Valley Railway in 1920, whilst no. 16 was scrapped post-Grouping.

Opposite above **STEAM RAIL MOTOR – NO. 7**
In April 1904 six steam rail motors were ordered from Swindon Works. This was the second batch and differed from the first two in having curved front ends, modified roof design and enlarged windows. No. 7 was the penultimate steam rail motor in the order and had seating for a total of 54 persons.

Opposite middle **STEAM RAIL MOTOR – NO. 43**
By 1905, a 70 ft coach body was favoured in order to increase seating capacities. No. 43 was amongst 14 erected in the year to the new design, which included improving the bogie, brakes and modifying the interior.

Opposite below **STEAM RAIL MOTOR – NO. 1**
Costs were always under scrutiny by the railways. Many branch lines across the country were loss-making and attempts to remedy this included the introduction of steam rail motors at the start of the 20th century. Introduced by the London & South Western Railway, these consisted of a steam engine fitted inside a carriage, creating a single, cheaper unit. The GWR was soon to take interest in the concept and their own steam rail motor, no. 1, was built in October 1903. The unit and sister no. 2 were distinct from later examples by having flat ends amongst some other detail differences.

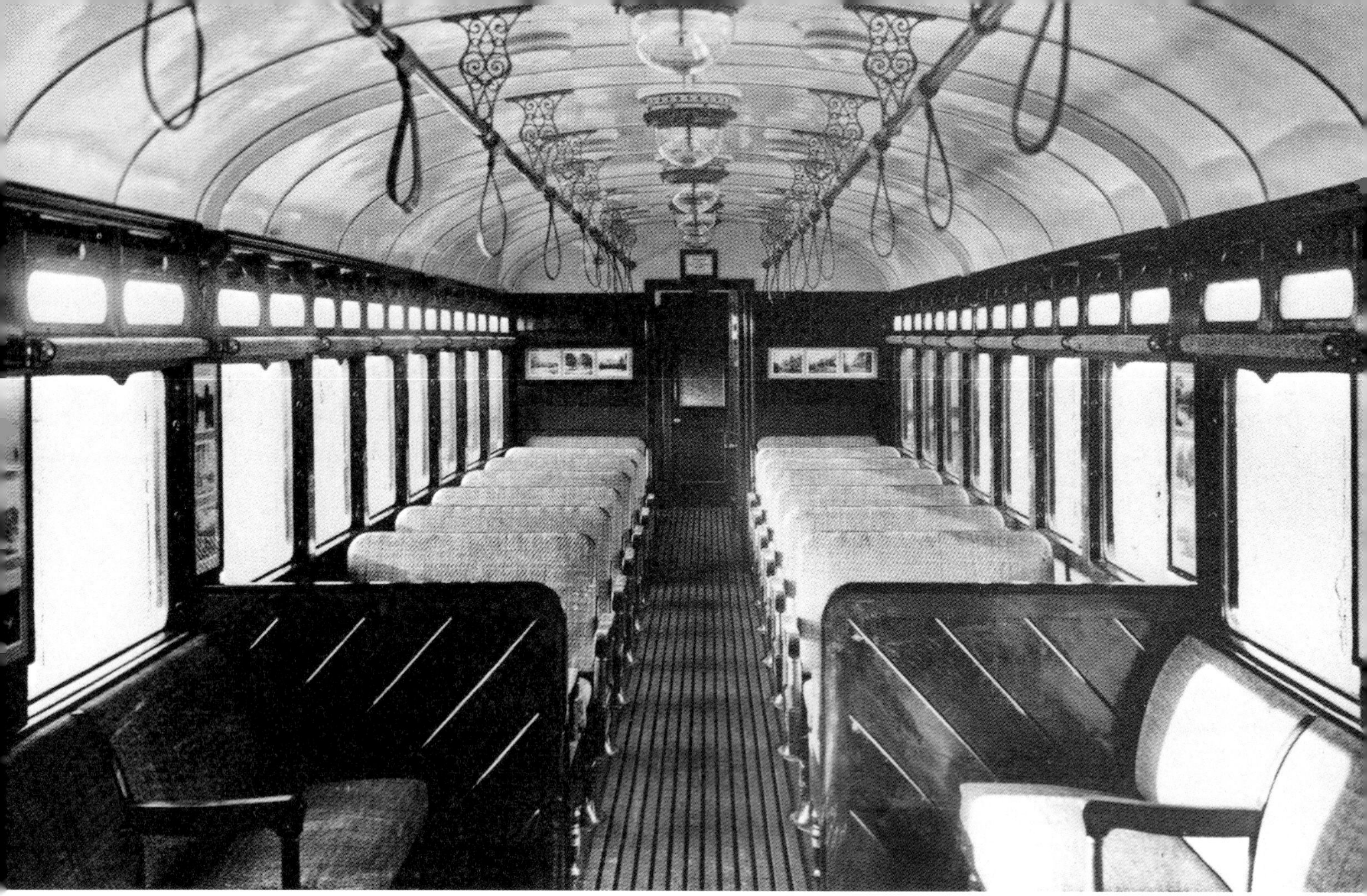

Above **STEAM RAIL MOTOR TRAILER – NO. 4**
With the success of the GWR's steam rail motors, the company decided to build extra units without steam engines for increased capacity. The first was built at Swindon in 1904 and more followed. No. 4 was built in 1905 following experience with the first trailers in service. They were found to inhibit the performance of the steam rail motors and as a result a pair of trailers was coupled to an 0-4-2T locomotive. This saw both ends of the trailer equipped for auto-train working.

Opposite above **STEAM RAIL MOTOR – NO. 43**
A view of the interior from steam rail motor no. 43, looking from the vestibule end to the main seating area, smoking compartment and boiler room/operating compartment.

Opposite below **STEAM RAIL MOTOR – NO. 1**
The Cheltenham & Great Western Union Railway was promoted in the 1830s to join Cheltenham with Gloucester and Swindon. Yet, the company had financial difficulties and could only complete the section from Swindon to Cirencester. The GWR stepped in to take over and completed the remainder in the mid-1840s. In 1903, steam rail motor no. 1 was placed in service on the route, running between Stonehouse station and Chalford station. No. 1 is at the first mentioned in this image from 1903.

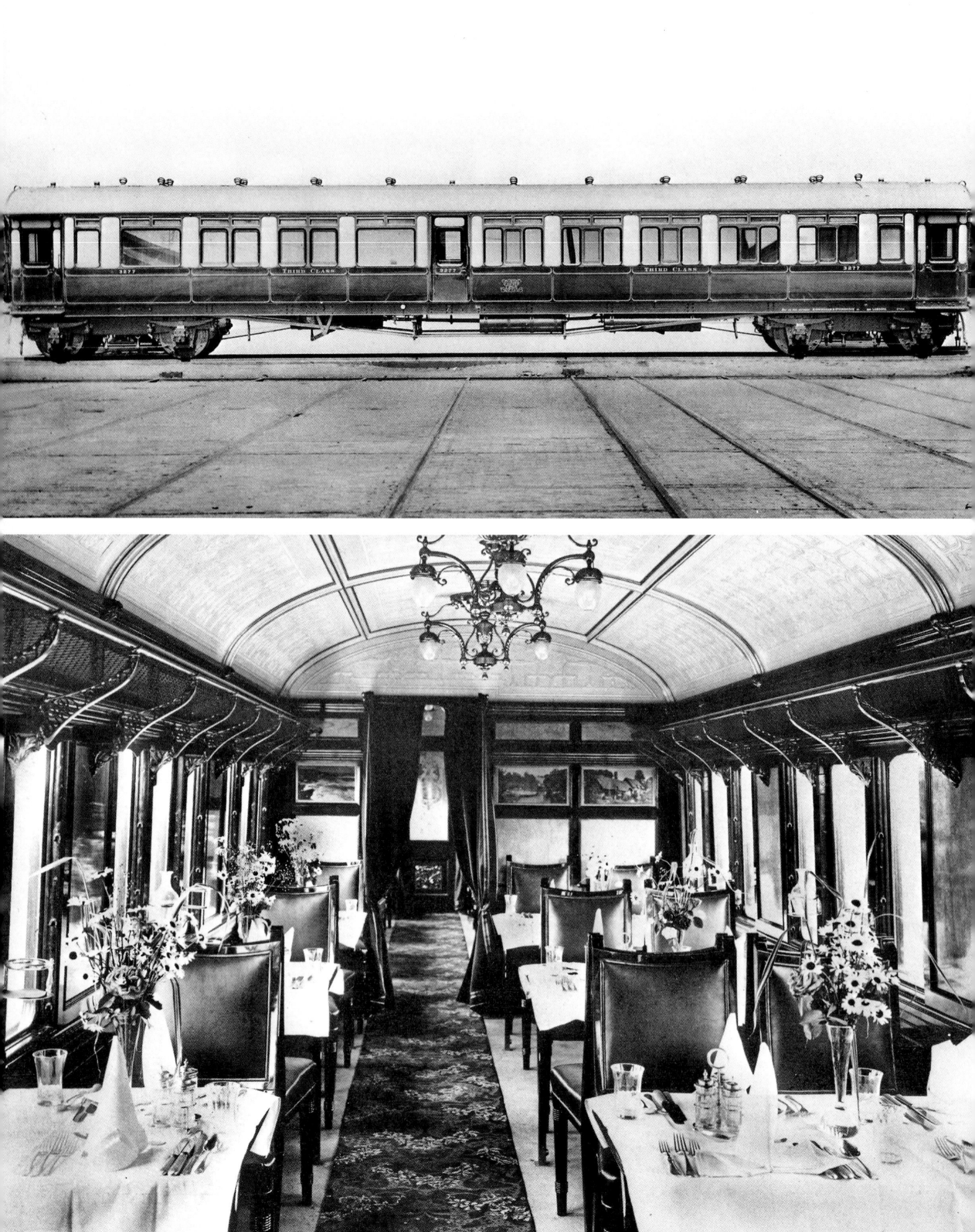

Above **CONCERTINA DINING CARRIAGE**
Lots 1114, 1115 and 1118 covered the construction of two designs of second-class dining carriages in 1906. After 30 years, the units were refreshed and no. 9527 was amongst those, being pictured here after the transformation work in 1936.

Opposite above **THIRD-CLASS CARRIAGE**
Third-class Dreadnought carriage no. 3277 was built in 1905. An unusual feature of these was that the corridor ran halfway along one side, then changed over to the other. This was done with the reasoning of better weight distribution and the nine compartments were split five to four. The corridors were partitioned off from the vestibules by sliding doors. Third-class Dreadnought coaches had red upholstery, whilst the first-class compartments were green.

Opposite below **CONCERTINA DINING CARRIAGE**
The Dreadnought stock was said to be unpopular with travellers who were used to having a door for each individual compartments. Therefore in 1906/1907 some new stock appeared with the same width bodies, 9 ft, yet the doors had to be recessed in order that the door handles did not foul the loading gauge. This gave rise to the sobriquet Concertina to describe the stock. Though the dining carriage did not look like the compartment stock, owing to the year of production the vehicle has been grouped in that series. The interior of a dining carriage is illustrated here and a noticeable change from earlier stock is the switch from fixed bench seats to chairs.

92   THE GLORIOUS YEARS OF THE GWR – CARRIAGES

Above **COMPOSITE SLEEPING CARRIAGE**

For the Paddington to Neyland service, composite sleeping carriage no. 9093 was built in 1919. During the war years, the vehicle was rebuilt as a first-class sleeper and included in a special train formed for use by General Dwight D. Eisenhower.

Opposite above **FUNERAL CARRIAGE**

In the 19th century and up to around the 1980s, the transportation of the dead around the country by rail was a normal occurrence. At the turn of the century, the coffin was charged one shilling per mile and had to travel more than ten miles on the GWR's system. Many deceased important persons were also moved by the railways. In this instance, the Royal saloon has been specially decorated and fitted for the final journey of Queen Victoria from Paddington to Windsor for her interment. This occurred on 2nd February 1901 with departure at 13.42. The Royal Train in this instance expanded to eight carriages hauled by Atbara Class 4-4-0 no. 3373 *Atbara* which was temporarily renamed *Royal Sovereign* for the day. In the Royal saloon, the Queen was accompanied by the Duke of Norfolk, Duke of Portland, Earl of Clarendon and Earl of Pembroke.

Opposite below **SLEEPING CARRIAGE**

Another design completed as part of the Dreadnought series was the diagram J6 sleeping carriage. Built in 1907, the body was placed on two six-wheel bogies and contained ten berths with another being a double berth. There were also two lavatories and an attendant's compartment. Four sleeping cars were completed and these ran until condemned during 1936.

Opposite above **STEAM AUTO TRAIN**
Whilst the rail motor was being introduced in the early 20th century, the GWR continued normal practice of using an 0-4-2T and single carriage on branch services. In two instances, the locomotives were enclosed in coachwork. Armstrong 517 Class no. 833 was one, being converted in 1906 and running like this to 1911. The engine is seen here in 1914 with a pair of third-class and two third-class brake carriages forming an auto train.

Opposite below **QUEEN'S SALOON**
Built in 1897, the Queen's saloon is seen in 1909. The carriage remained part of the Royal Train to 1930 and was subsequently preserved. Currently the coach is displayed at STEAM, Swindon.

Below **LUGGAGE VAN**
In 1914 a group of thirds, brake thirds and luggage vans were ordered from Swindon. Amongst these was no. 261. Some of the carriages later saw use in ambulance trains for service in Europe.

Bottom **COMPOSITE BRAKE CARRIAGE**
Just before the First World War a number of composite brake carriages were completed. Two versions of the design existed where one, diagram F20, was fitted to work as a slip coach. No. 6945 is seen and was not equipped for this.

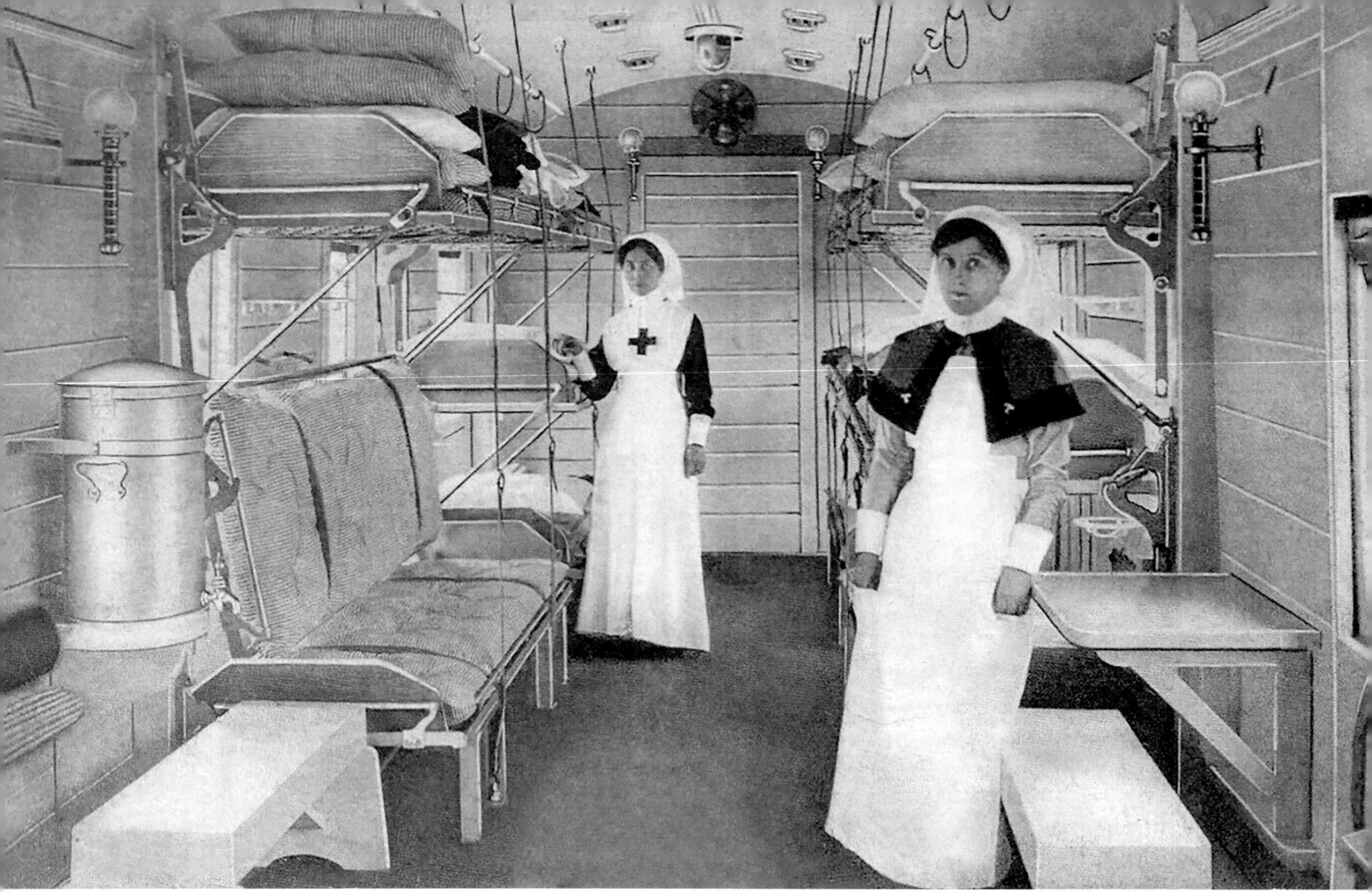

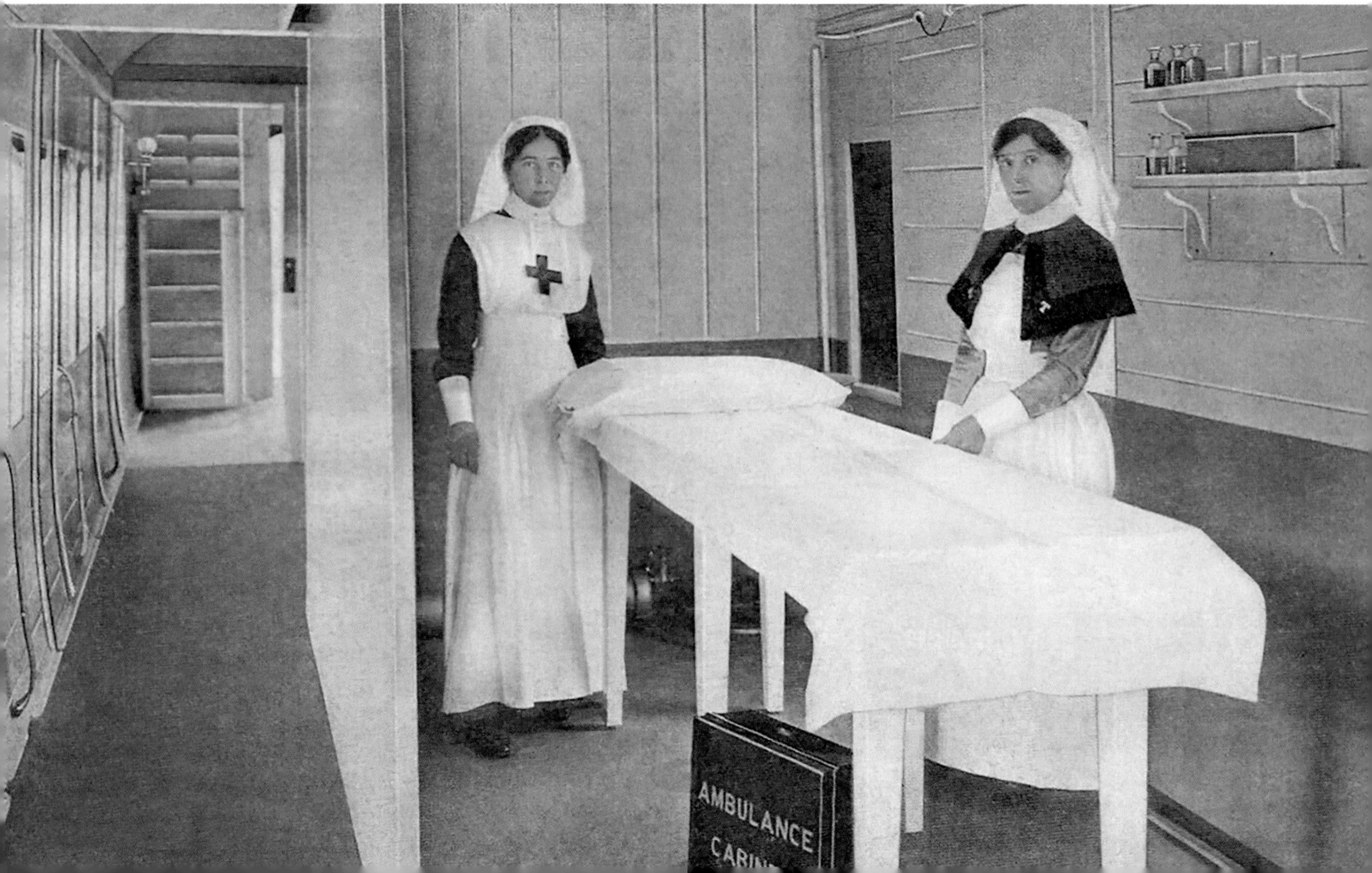

Opposite and above **AMBULANCE TRAIN**
At the outbreak of the First World War, the railways in Britain were placed under Government control for the duration of the conflict. The GWR was affected through the loss of men to the Armed Forces and a change in focus to assisting the war effort. At Swindon Works the attention switched to munitions work, such as high explosive shells, guns, gun carriages, and construction of road wagons, as well as ambulance trains. This trio of images show some of the rooms used in ambulance train no. 18 built at Swindon in 1915. This had sixteen carriages in total with accommodation for 482 patients (320 sitting and 144 laid). The staff consisted of 45, with 32 orderlies, 6 cooks, 4 nurses and three surgeons. In August 1915, the train was exhibited to the public at Paddington station and for a donation to the War Fund, people could view the carriages.

Top **THIRD-CLASS BRAKE CARRIAGE**
In 1924, six corridor third-class brake vehicles were built to diagram H24. There were four compartments in the 70 ft body, with a guard's compartment and luggage area taking the remaining 40 ft.

Above **ARTICULATED TRIPLET CARRIAGE SET**
In the early 20th century, the relatively swift switch from six wheels to four-wheel bogies left many older coaches noticeably outdated. On the Great Northern Railway, Carriage and Wagon Superintendent H.N. Gresley decided to place redundant six-wheel carriages on bogies but in sets of two, three, four, etc. Whilst he went on to find further success with this idea in the Silver Jubilee and Coronation carriage sets of the 1930s, other British railways shunned the idea. In the mid-1920s, the GWR tested the articulation of carriages with 18 coaches joined into sets of three. These comprised brake third, third and composite carriage and were used on suburban services. A main line set was built subsequently with two triplets and a twin forming an eight-carriage train. This consisted of a brake third, third, third, then a restaurant dining car triplet and lastly there was a first and brake first. The third-class carriages are pictured here. The experiment lasted for around a decade before conversion to standard occurred.

Opposite above **RESTAURANT CARRIAGE**
Six 70 ft dining carriages were built at Swindon at the eve of Grouping. The interior of no. 9561 is seen here showing three of the body's sections. The exterior was notable as having no decoration. Post-Second World War, the group was refurbished.

Opposite below **THIRD BRAKE CARRIAGE**
Before the First World War, the GWR was to carry out a suburban stock renewal. The company had to wait until the early 1920s to enact this proposal. A large number of third-class and third brake carriages were part of the programme, with no. 4704 of the latter design which numbered 52.

Above and opposite **FIRST-CLASS BRAKE SALOON**
These two interiors are from one of two first-class brake saloons built at Swindon in 1930 to diagram G59. The carriages were made available to private parties on request and featured a dining saloon accommodating 14, a compartment and another saloon for eight. Kitchen facilities were also provided and there was a guard's room. An unusual feature of the coaches was windows in the ends of the carriage. Both were refurbished following the war and no. 9005 was rebuilt in 1961, lasting to 1974. No. 9004 was condemned in 1963 and has been preserved.

Above SUPER SALOON
In 1928 the GWR made the decision to test the use of Pullman carriages on the West Country expresses. Arriving for the summer season of 1929, eight carriages formed a train running from Paddington to Plymouth for ship traffic. From July 1929, the set was redeployed as the 'Torquay Pullman Limited'. This returned the following summer but proved a failure and the set was sent to the Southern Railway. The lack of success was down to high costs of hiring the coaches from the Pullman Company and instead the GWR decided to build their own luxurious carriages. These were over 61 ft long and 9 ft 7 in. wide. Owing to their prestige, the vehicles were named after the Royal Family and no. 9113 *Prince of Wales*, is seen here when new in 1931. The set went on to be used for special occasions to the 1960s and five have been preserved.

Opposite above COMPOSITE CARRIAGE
Diagram E31 consisted of 56 non-corridor composite carriages for use in suburban services. These were built from 1927 to 1929, with no. 9237 being completed towards the end of production. The bodies were just over 58 ft long and had nine compartments split four to first class and five to third. The first compartments were 6 ft 9 in. wide and the third were a foot shorter.

Opposite below FIRST-CLASS DINING CARRIAGE
A view inside the first-class dining carriage built as part of the triplet articulated set in mid-1925. The body was 50 ft long, with 6 ft wide sections and seating provided to 42 passengers.

Above **SUPER SALOON**
The interior of the super saloon is shown here. There were two saloon areas, one 14 ft 6 in., another 21 ft 9 in. For the latter, seating was arranged to three sets of four chairs on one side and two sets of two with a single on the other. The smaller area had four sets of two seats whilst there was also a four-seat coupé compartment. Lavatories were located at either end.

Opposite **COMPOSITE CARRIAGE**
By the end of the 1920s, 70 ft carriages were out of favour and the designs moved to a length of 60 ft. A number of new coaches appeared at this time, including fresh sets for the 'Cornish Riviera Express'. Part of the train was a composite carriage and the interior of a third-class compartment is seen here. There were a total of seven in the vehicle split three to third class and four to first class. Seventeen carriages were constructed in 1929/1930 to diagram E137.

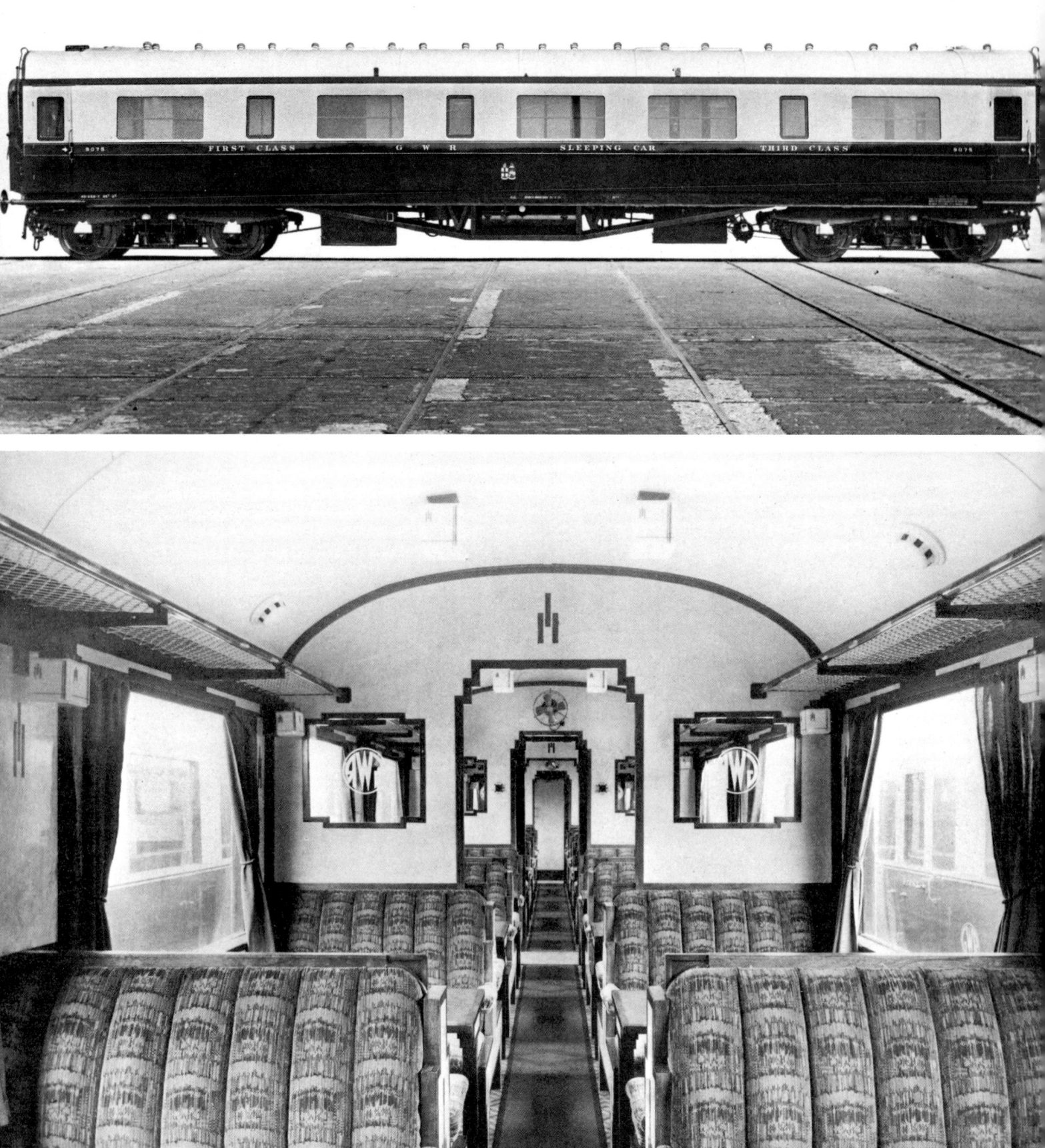

Above **THIRD-CLASS RESTAURANT CARRIAGE**
At first the excursion sets did not have a dedicated restaurant carriage as meals were expected to be served at seats. This soon proved impractical to carry food through several coaches. Two restaurant carriages were built to diagram H48 to remedy the issue.

Opposite above **COMPOSITE SLEEPING CARRIAGE**
Whereas several examples of first- and third-class sleeping carriages were built in the late 1920s/early 1930s, only one composite sleeping carriage appeared, no. 9075. The coach was constructed to diagram J13 in 1931. Three compartments were third class and a feature of both the third class and composite was the lack of attendant facilities for travellers.

Opposite below **THIRD-CLASS SALOON CARRIAGE**
In the mid-1930s the GWR built dedicated trains for excursions. These saw the adoption of the centre aisle for the third-class saloon and saloon brake. The interior of the saloon is shown here.

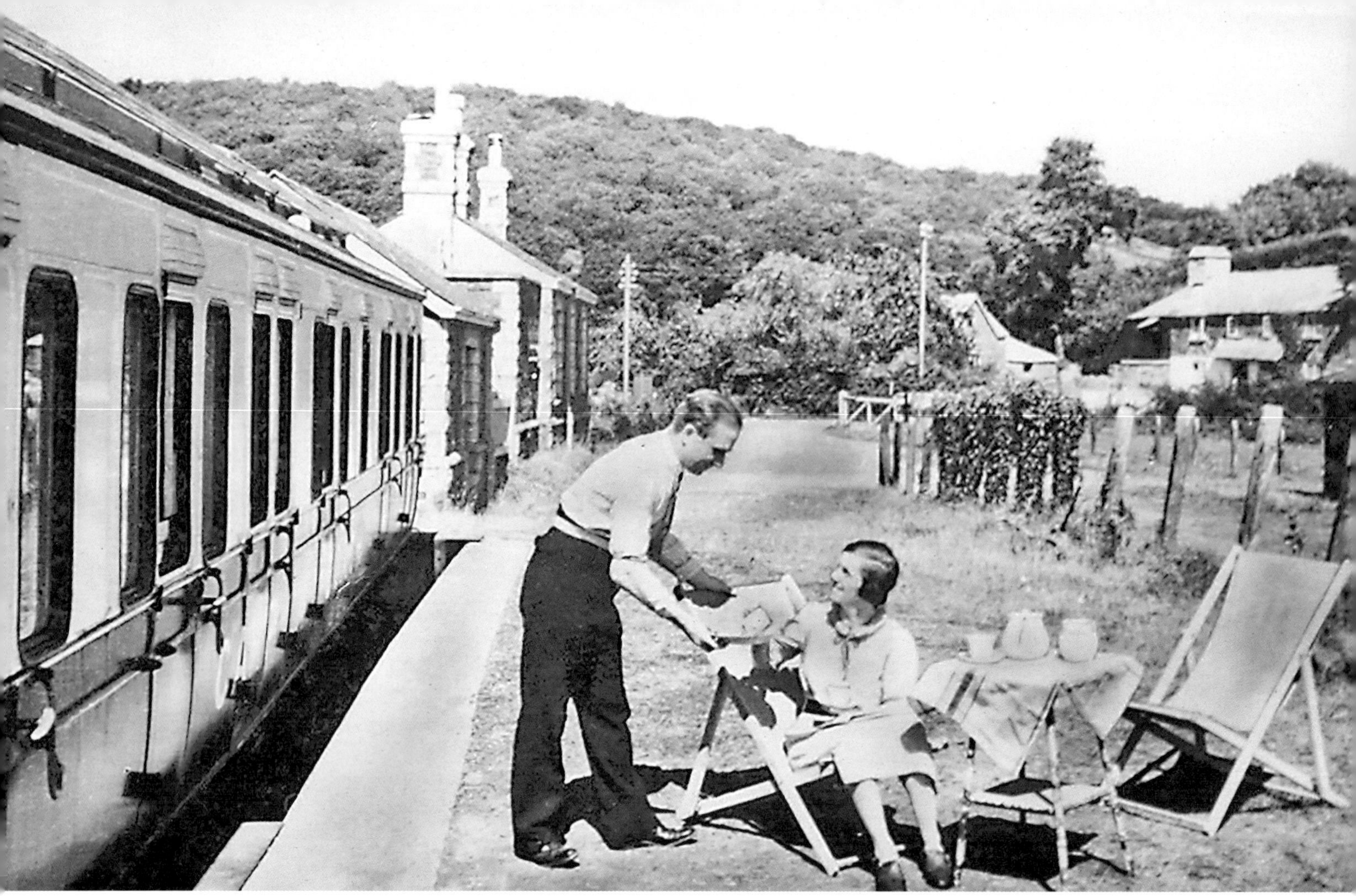

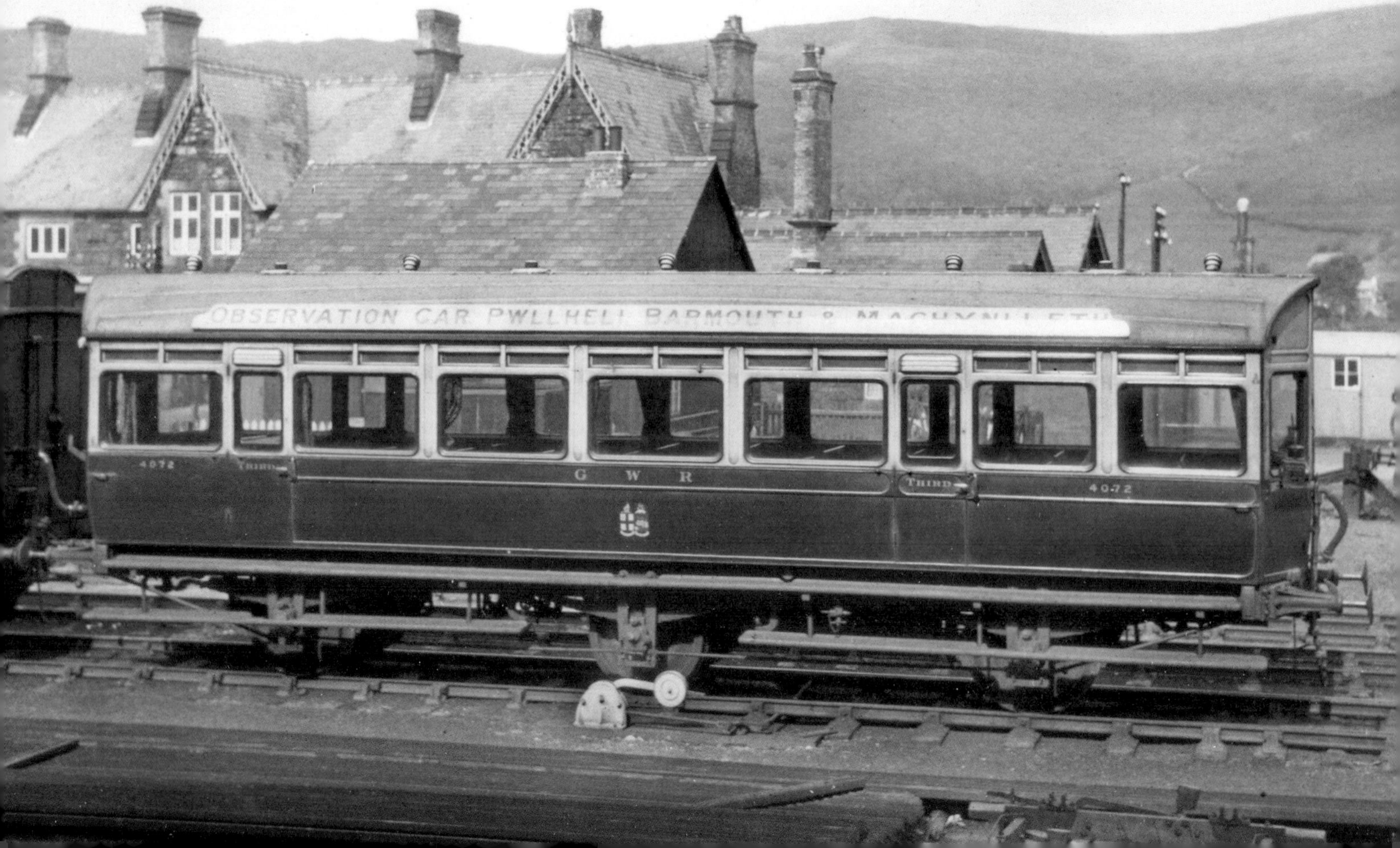
OBSERVATION CAR PWLLHELI BARMOUTH & MACHYNLLETH
4072
THIRD
G W R
THIRD
4072

Above **THIRD-CLASS RESTAURANT CARRIAGE**
For the new 'Cornish Riviera Express' train of 1935 the kitchen was combined with the first-class dining area. Third-class passengers were served in their own carriage of which two were built to diagram H44. No. 9637 is one and had two seats either side of the gangway and the two saloons each had seating for 32 passengers.

Opposite above **CAMP COACH**
The London & North Eastern Railway was the first company to introduce camping coaches in 1933. This saw redundant coaching stock repurposed as accommodation for holidaymakers and placed in picturesque locations. The venture proved successful and in the following year both the London Midland & Scottish Railway and GWR began offering similar facilities. Nineteen coaches started the venture and developed to 65 examples in the summer before the Second World War. The price for a week was around £5.

Opposite below **OBSERVATION SALOON**
In the late 1910s, the Cambrian Railways built two observation saloons for use on the coastal route between Machynlleth and Pwllheli. The GWR continued to operate the pair until 1936.

Above **THIRD-CLASS RESTAURANT CARRIAGE**
A view inside the third-class restaurant carriage forming part of the 'Cornish Riviera Express' train of 1935.

Opposite **KITCHEN CARRIAGE**
The 'Cornish Riviera Express' was introduced in 1904 and became a particularly important service for the GWR and many of the primary carriage developments were first used in the train's formation. As the company approached the centenary year, a new set of coaches for the 'Cornish Riviera Express' was deemed desirable and followed the lead of the super saloons. Where the group deviated was the kitchen as a separate carriage and saloons ran in the formation previously, now the kitchen was paired with a first-class saloon. At 60 ft long, the carriage allowed 14 ft for the kitchen and just over 26 ft to the saloon, which could seat 24 persons. This view was taken in the kitchen looking to the stove that used gas. Two vehicles were built to diagram H43.

Above **COMPOSITE BRAKE CARRIAGE**
Between 1933 and 1936, 116 non-corridor composite brake carriages were constructed to diagram E147. These had six compartments, one first class and five third class, and luggage compartment. No. 6820 was part of this group but was later modified along similar lines to diagram A34. This had the same configuration though was new with an auto-train compartment.

Opposite above left **THIRD-CLASS BRAKE CARRIAGE**
The Burry Port & Gwendraeth Valley Railway began life as a canal undertaking which was converted to a railway in the 1860s. This was done with costs in mind and as a result the loading gauge was particularly restrictive. Though mainly a mineral line, passenger services were offered and in the late 1930s six new carriages were built, possessing significantly lower roofs than standard. The compartment in one of the brake thirds (diagram D129) is illustrated here.

Opposite above right **THIRD-CLASS CARRIAGE**
In 1938 and 1940 the GWR built a large number of third-class compartment carriages for main line services. These were to diagram C77 with 60 ft 11¼ in. bodies, eight compartments with 2 lavatories. There were four doors along the corridor side and the compartment side had two at the vestibule ends. Most survived to the mid-1960s and several have been preserved. The compartment of the C77 third-class carriage is seen here.

Opposite below **THIRD-CLASS BRAKE CARRIAGE**
A set of six corridor third-class brake carriages to diagram D120 was built in 1935 as part of the new stock programme. These only had two compartments, one smoking the other non-smoking, with a guard's room and luggage compartment, which was 33 ft 7 in. long. The passenger compartments were 6 ft 3 in. long by 6 ft 10 in. wide which was slightly shorter but wider than other contemporary GWR third-class carriages.

Above **SPECIAL SALOON**

In 1940, two special 12-wheel saloons were constructed to diagram G62 for use by special persons during the Second World War. There was a saloon, dining saloon, coupé compartment, kitchen and pantry. Nos 9001 and 9002 were in service to the late 1960s and have been preserved.

Opposite **SUPER SALOON**

Super saloon no. 9111 *King George* was built to diagram G20, as was no. 9112 *Queen Mary*. The two carriages were decorated by Trollope & Sons using matched walnut burr panelling as well as French-polished walnut. A 10-shilling supplement was applicable to the first-class fare for travel in the super saloon which was used on boat trains and race specials. Withdrawn in 1967, no. 9111 was preserved by the South Devon Railway Association and is currently in service.

Above **THIRD-CLASS CARRIAGE**
The GWR built around 200 carriages in 1940, falling to 100 in 1941, then transitioning to war work up to the end of the war. In the mid-1940s thoughts turned to renewing coaching stock under F.W. Hawksworth, who replaced Charles Collett as CME in 1941. The new building programme included corridor third-class carriages to diagram C82. The design was slightly modified from earlier coaches of the type in having larger bodies at 64 ft, though still with eight compartments. Seating was for 64 passengers. The interior of a compartment is seen here.

Opposite above left **FIRST-CLASS SLEEPING CARRIAGE**
Nine diagram J12 first-class sleeping carriages were constructed between 1929 and 1930. This image from 1946 shows the interior of a berth in no. 9066 which was built in 1930. Note the raised top of the sink, which was covered when not used and acted as a table. The J12s were in service to the early 1960s. The GWR planned new sleeping carriages post-war, yet the scheme was not realised until the early 1950s when built by British Railways.

Opposite above right **SLIP CARRIAGE**
The use of slip coaches lasted on the GWR for just over 100 years, from the first test slip in 1858 to the introduction at the end of the year and the last slip on 10th September 1960. The early advantage of the practice was reduction of journey times by eliminating stops yet this came at a greater cost by the need for extra staff, whilst also inconveniencing passengers that wished to use other facilities as slip coaches were nearly always isolated from the main train. Nevertheless, the GWR had as many as 79 slip coaches before the First World War but this number gradually declined during the inter-war period. The lever for the slip coupling is seen here and the release of the lever freed a wedge allowing the hinged drawhook to fall. The carriage, either with one or two other carriages attached, then fell away from the main train as the vacuum brakes were activated.

Opposite below **THIRD-CLASS CARRIAGE**
An exterior view of a diagram C82 third-class carriage, in this instance no. 783.

TRAIN PIPE
G.W.R.
NOTICE.
66CF
BY ORDER

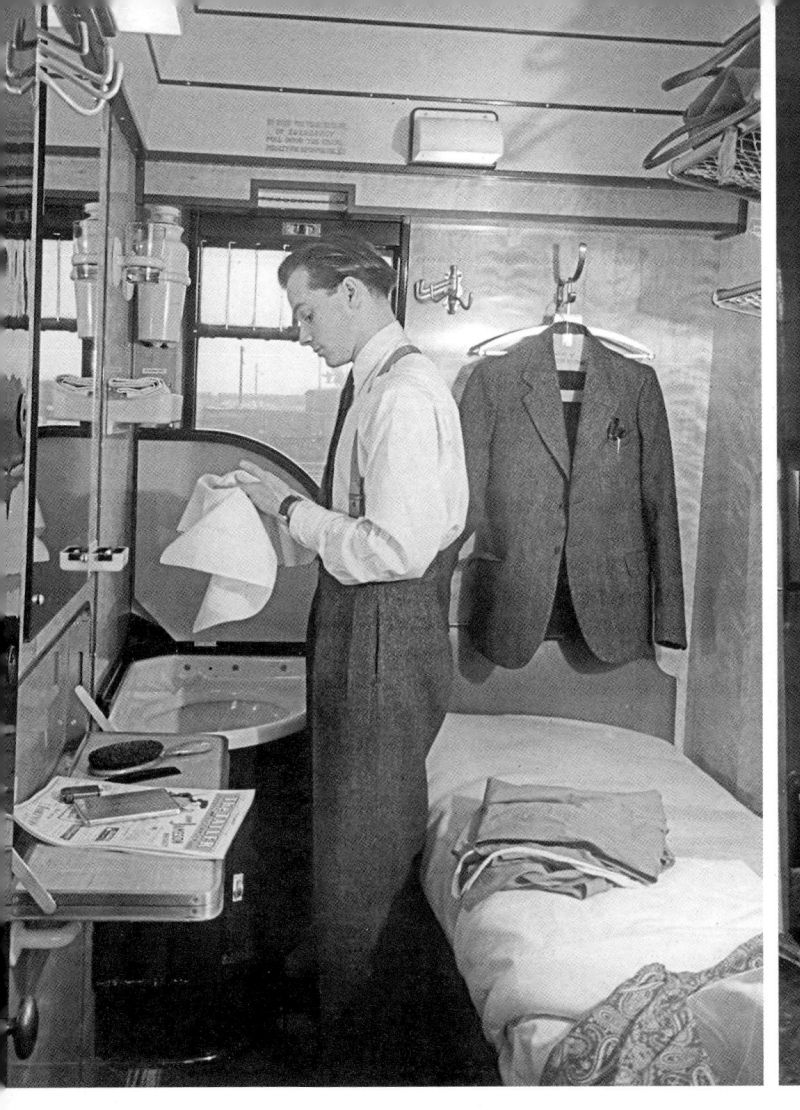

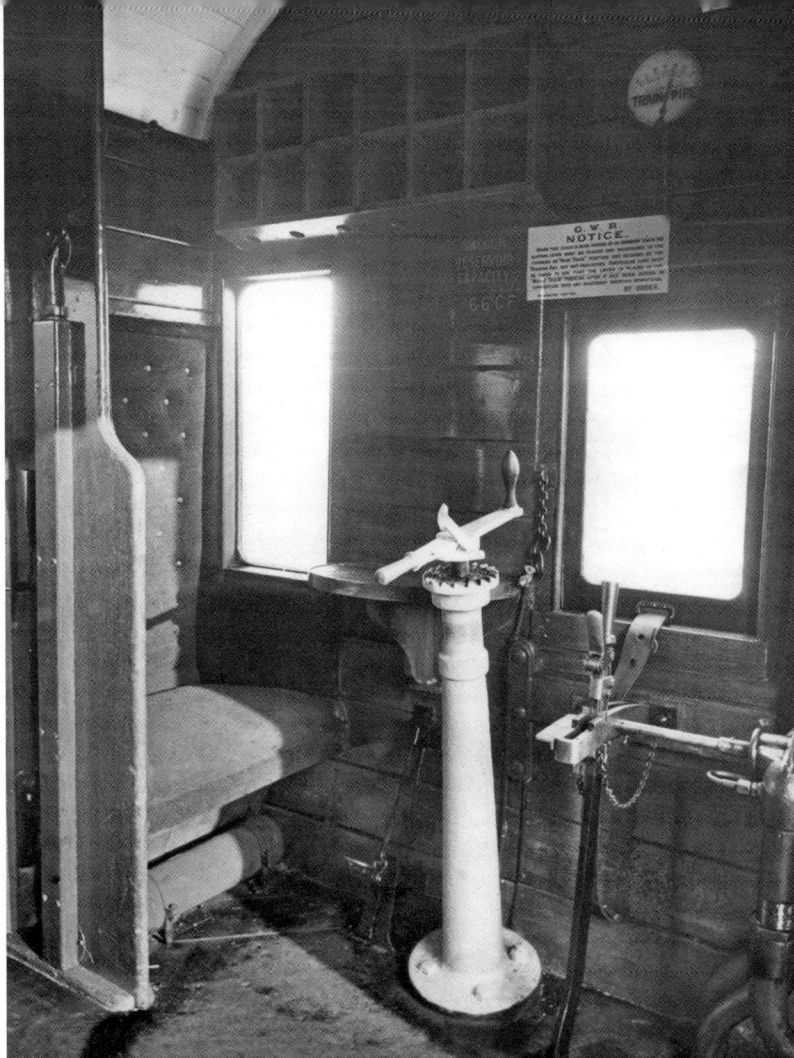

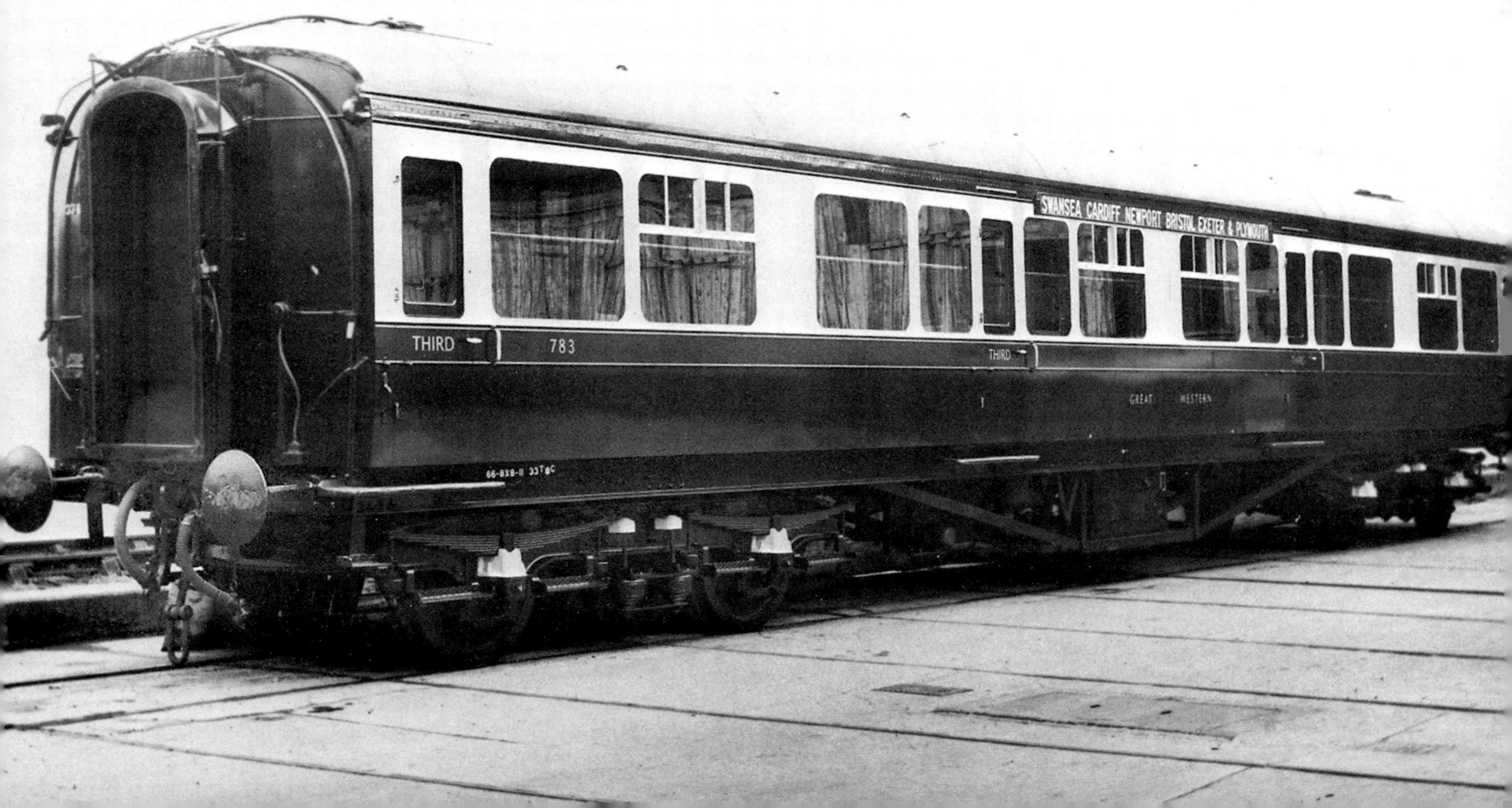
SWANSEA CARDIFF NEWPORT BRISTOL EXETER & PLYMOUTH
THIRD
783
THIRD
GREAT WESTERN

BUSES

Above **MILNES DAIMLER DOUBLE-DECK OMNIBUS**
Milnes Daimler was formed in the early 20th century as Milnes branched into the new road motor vehicle business by importing chassis from Daimler in Germany and fitting these with bodies as requirements dictated. The company supplied a number of 20 horsepower vehicles to the GWR following the introduction of buses. No. 7 is working the Marlborough to Calne service during October 1904.

Opposite above **MILNES DAIMLER OPEN BUS**
The prospect of spending £85,000 on a light railway between Halston and The Lizard did not appeal to the GWR in mid-1903. The company decided to trial a motor omnibus service owing to a local scheme branching into the area at the time. Two Milnes Daimler vehicles were purchased and went into service on 17th August 1903. Originally open topped, the GWR converted the pair to have a roof and the bus is seen in this form around the start of the service. Finding success, the buses ran to late 1904 when road conditions halted the operations.

Opposite below **CLARKSON STEAM OMNIBUS**
For the Wolverhampton to Bridgnorth bus service, three Clarkson steam omnibuses were placed in service for 7th November 1904. Experiencing problems, the vehicles were replaced, though they found further use elsewhere before sold to outside companies. No. 36 is pictured at Bridgnorth station.

Above **MOTOR BUS ACCIDENT**
On 13th December 1916 a GWR motor bus had a mishap on Solva Hill, east of St David's, Dyfed, Wales. The cause of the accident was the road which was icy and when Driver Horton applied the brakes, the bus skidded hitting the side of the road. The vehicle then moved to the other side and overturned. Both passengers and driver were shaken but thankfully uninjured.

Opposite above **BURFORD D BUS**
The South Wales Railway was originally to extend to Fishguard when built for ferry crossings to Ireland. Yet, the plans changed and Neyland was the end of the line. Independent companies eventually ran northward to Fishguard though by a longer route than necessary. In 1906, the GWR shortened the distance, laying a line from Clarbeston Road to Letterston. This initially had no stations and halts were added subsequently. Known initially as Mathry, Mathry Road Halt opened on 1st August 1923 and was active to April 1964. The station was the closest point to the cathedral city of St David's and this bus has presumably originated elsewhere and is travelling there via Mathry Halt. The vehicle is a Burford D 30 cwt chassis with single-deck body. H.G. Burford & Co. Ltd was founded by an ex-employee of Humber Ltd and director of Milnes Daimler in 1915 and went on to supply a range of motor vehicles.

Opposite below **MILNES DAIMLER BUS**
At Nether Stowey (between Bridgwater and Wilton), Milnes Daimler bus no. 20 pauses for this image to be captured, during the early 20th century. The vehicle began life as a single-deck unit with roof luggage rack in 1904. Subsequently, no. 20 has been converted to be a double-deck bus.

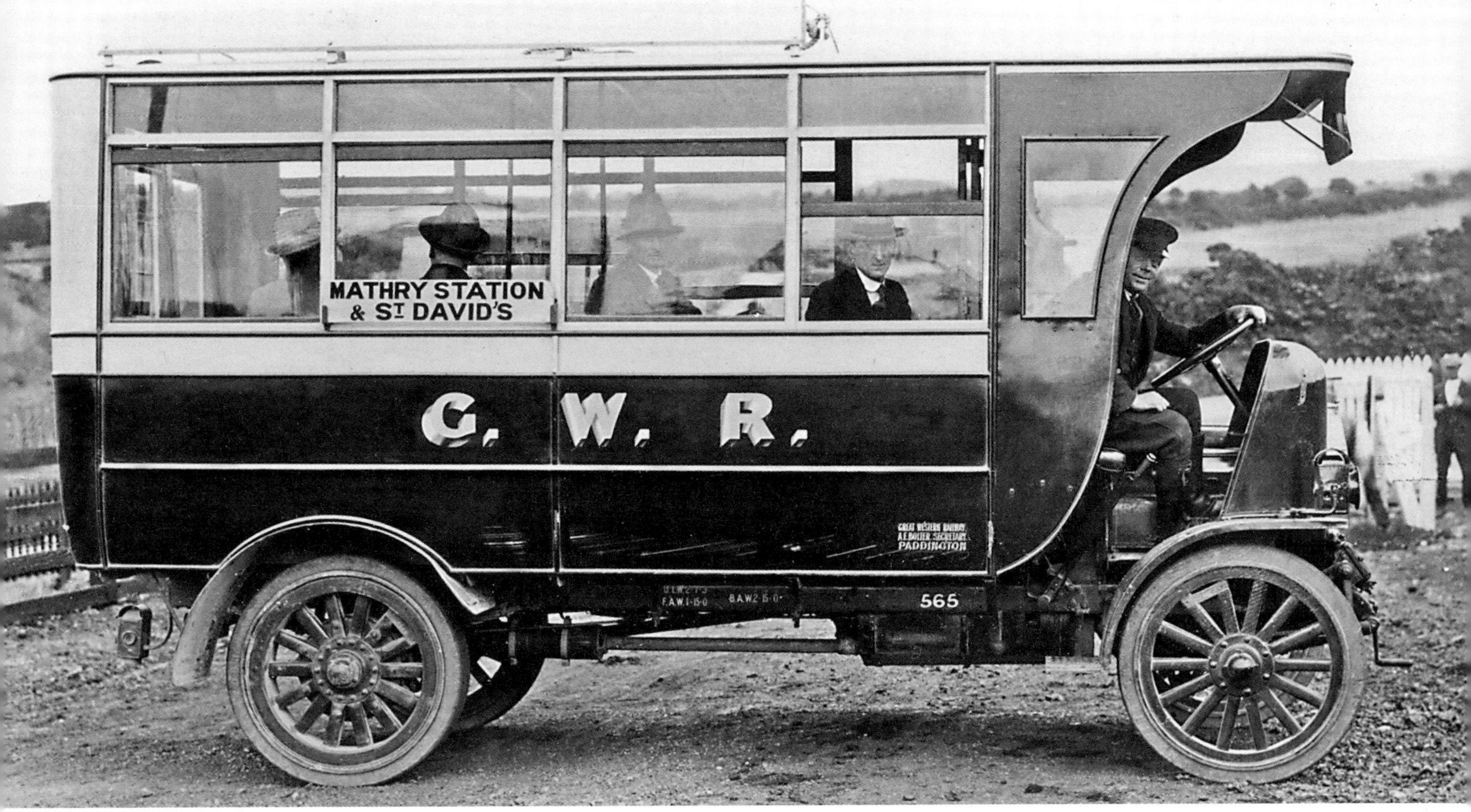
MATHRY STATION
& St DAVID'S
G. W. R.
PADDINGTON
565

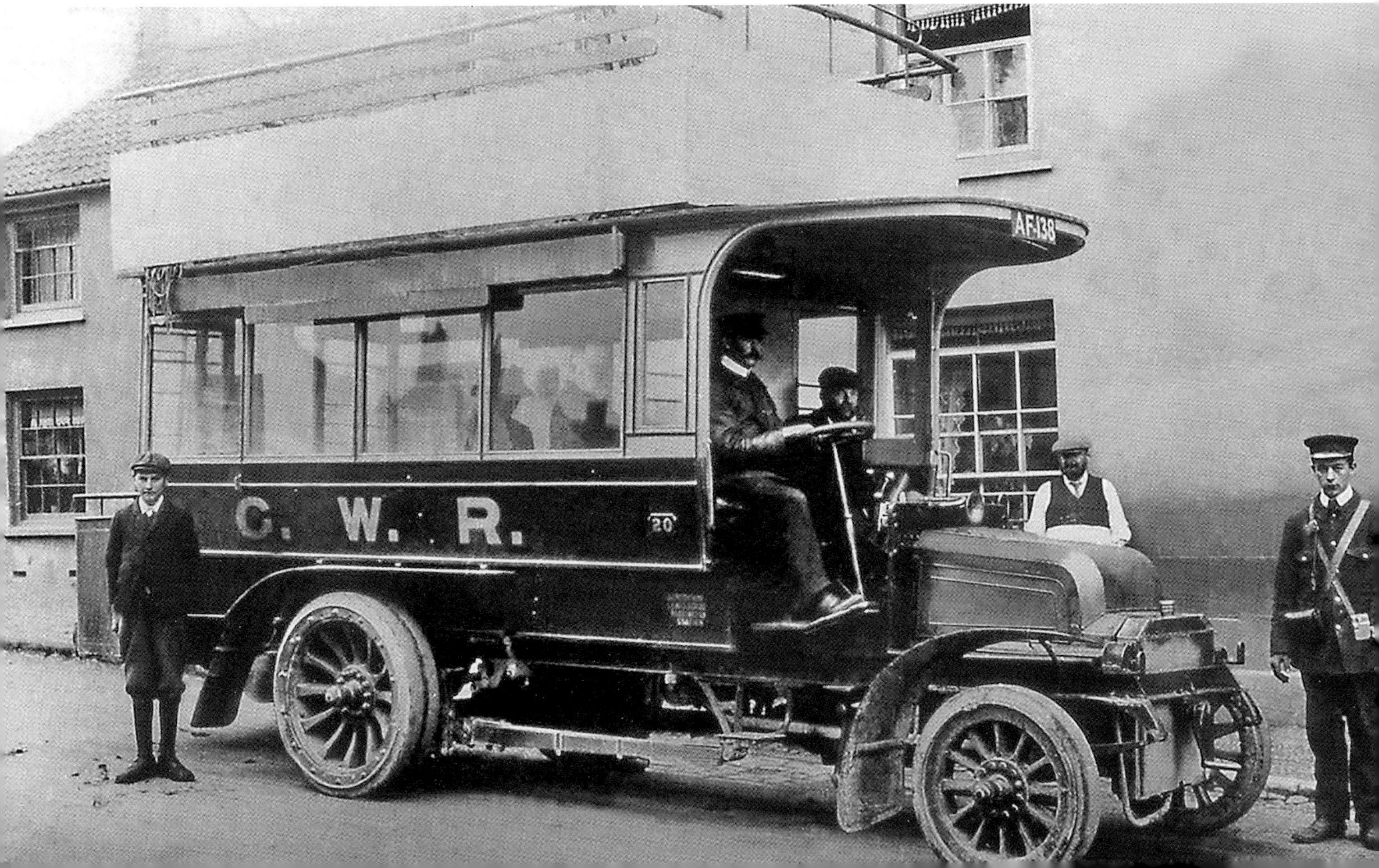
AF 138
G. W. R.
20

122 THE GLORIOUS YEARS OF THE GWR – BUSES

Above **MAUDSLAY/BUCKINGHAM COACH**
Improvements were made to the design of motor vehicles as the 1920s progressed, allowing the GWR to increase capacities of their buses. This led to the company offering land cruises which combined rail and road travel to interesting parts of areas served by the GWR. No. 1281 was built with a retractable roof as part of the land cruises which were offered in the summer months. In the winter, the coaches were repurposed as longer distance alternatives to the railway. No. 1281 had a chassis from the Maudslay Motor Co. and body built by John Buckingham Ltd, Birmingham.

Opposite above **GUY MOTORS BUS**
In September 1930, the GWR promoted a connecting bus service from Paddington station to Victoria for travellers to Europe using the South Coast boat trains. A Guy Motors 2-ton chassis was fitted with a single-deck body for 25 passengers. Two vehicles, nos 1650 and 1651, were in use to 1933 when the service transferred to London Transport. Both buses were converted into lorries at Swindon.

Opposite below **MILNES DAIMLER BUS**
The conductor of Milnes Daimler bus no. 8 helpfully illustrates the dual use of the vehicle. Though ten passengers could be carried on flip seats, the compartment also served a parcels and postal delivery role. Introduced in 1904 for The Lizard to Helston service, no. 8 is pictured at the latter station in that period.

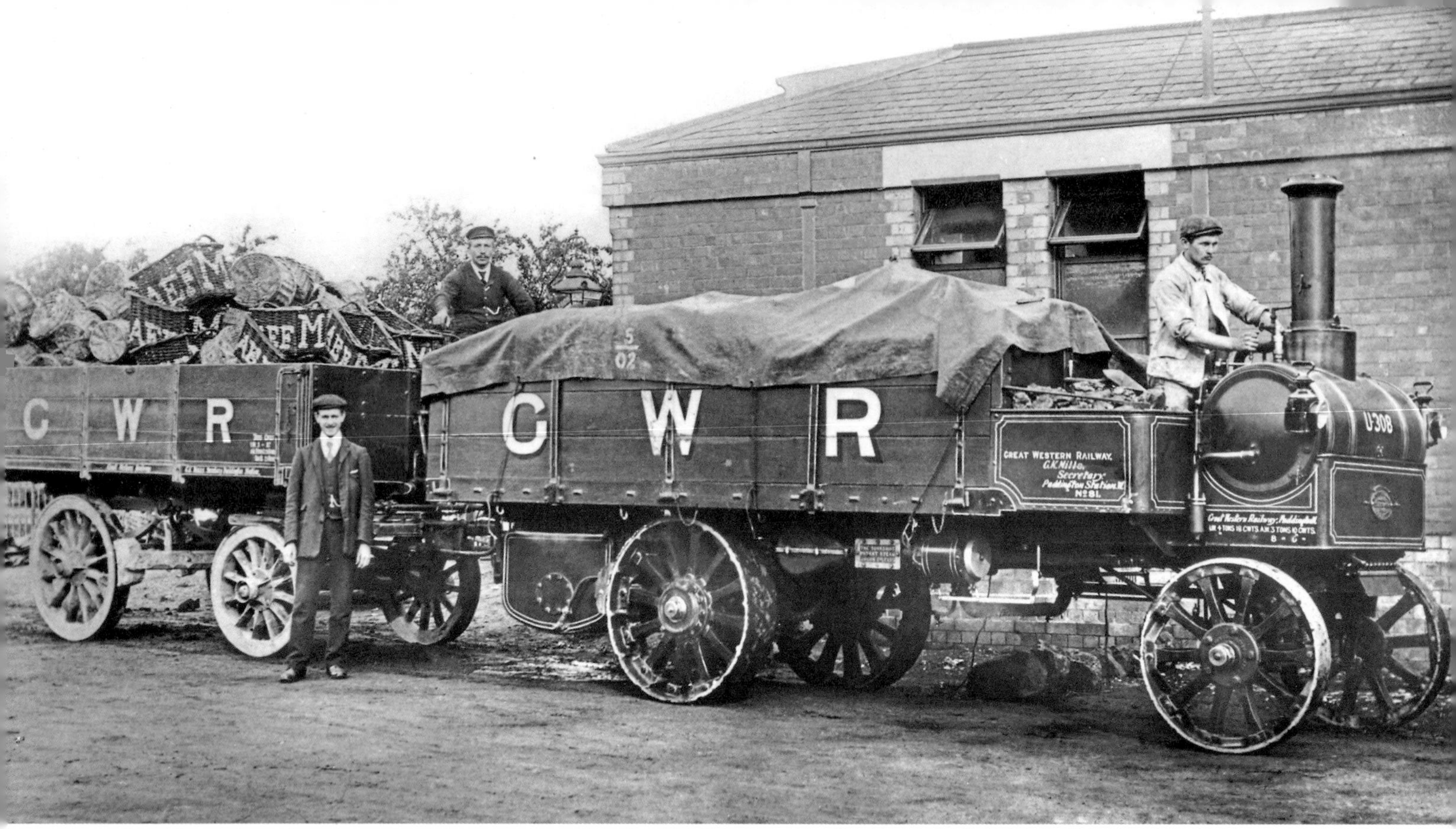
G W R
G W R
GREAT WESTERN RAILWAY.
U 308

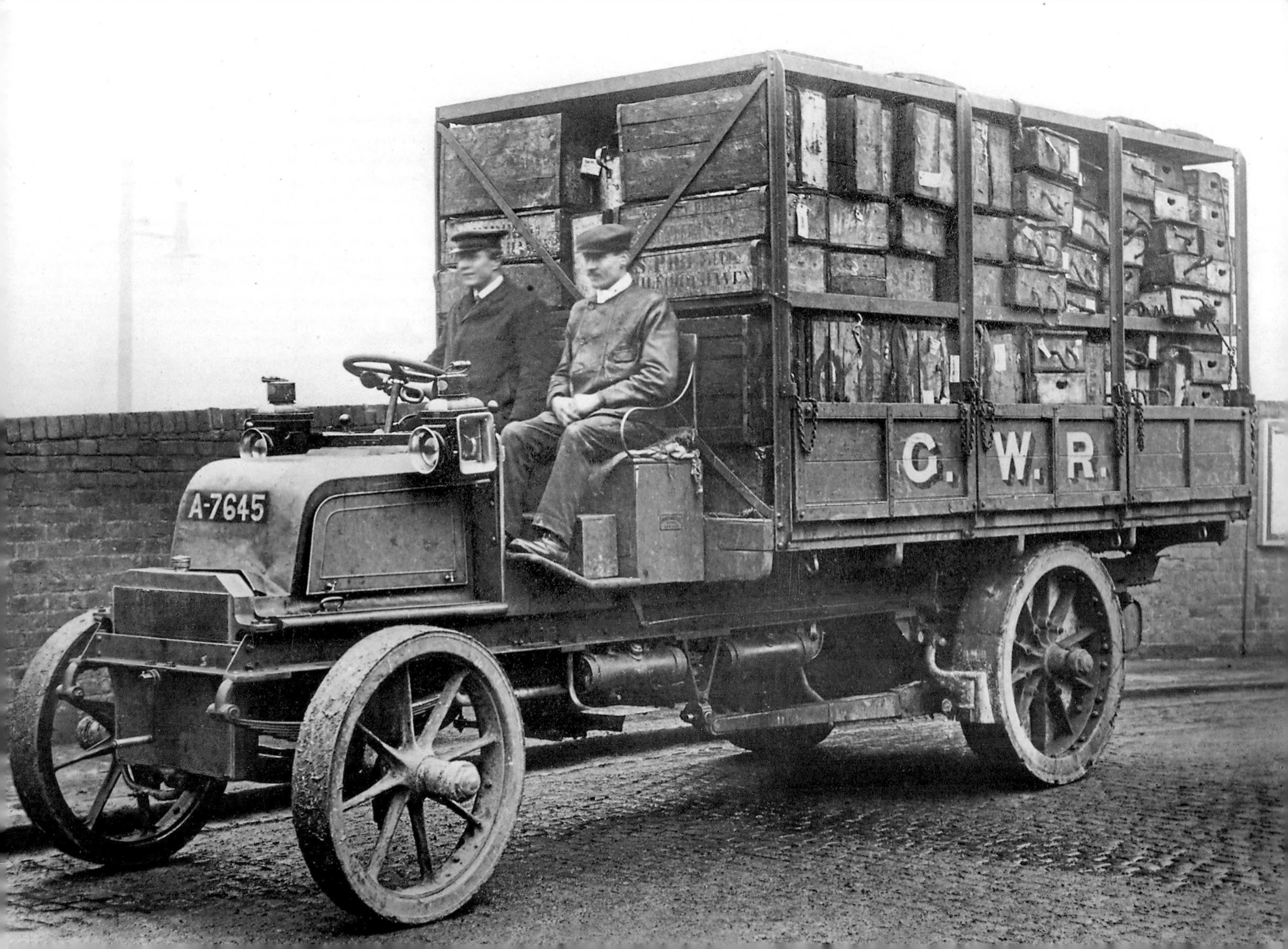
A-7645
G. W. R.

ROAD VEHICLES

Above **ELECTRIC LORRY**
The influence of American practices on the GWR also spread to the road vehicle department. Whilst in the country, officials inspected an electric lorry built by the Riker Electric Vehicle Co., New Jersey, and on the return to England, work was started on a GWR example. This appeared in 1906 and had two 80-volt electric motors capable of moving two tons. The battery had a range of 30 miles. The example pictured is the prototype whilst another example was constructed later.

Opposite above **STEAM LORRY AND TRAILER**
In 1902 Thornycroft Steam Wagon Company Ltd produced a steam lorry that was placed in several prominent trials. The GWR took notice and obtained a vehicle which was placed in service at Birmingham. The success of this led the company to further develop their motor fleet. An early example was this Yorkshire Patent Steam Wagon Co. Ltd four-ton steam lorry with trailer. The vehicle is pictured in mid-1905 and was used for vegetable traffic between the Teme Valley Agricultural Association and Henwick, Worcester.

Opposite below **MILNES DAIMLER LORRY**
The Milnes Daimler chassis was particularly adaptable and served the GWR in several areas during the early years of road haulage. In this instance, sides and a metal framework have been fitted so the vehicle could be used for fish traffic from Paddington to Billingsgate Market. The lorry had started life around 1904 as a flatbed but upgraded subsequently.

Above **FORD MODEL T LORRY**
On 1st October 1908 the Ford Motor Company began a revolution in transport with the introduction of the Model T automobile. This was mass produced on an assembly line with standard components, keeping costs down and allowing affordable prices when hitherto the price had been out of reach for many. The car was in constant production to 1927 when 15 million had been constructed. The design was not restricted to private operation and commercial vehicles were built using the chassis. Here, a flat body has been fitted to GWR lorry no. 331 which is seen at Paddington just before Grouping.

Opposite above **ELECTRIC LORRY**
In 1908 the GWR shops at Slough built an improved electric lorry. This was no. 95 and it is seen at work in the Paddington area. Note the advertising panel at the rear.

Opposite below **FODENS LTD STEAM LORRY**
For large-load haulage, the GWR obtained a 12-ton six-wheel steam lorry from Fodens Ltd. Placed in service in the Exeter area, no. S18 has a load of grain here in late 1929. Further vehicles ordered had body variations.

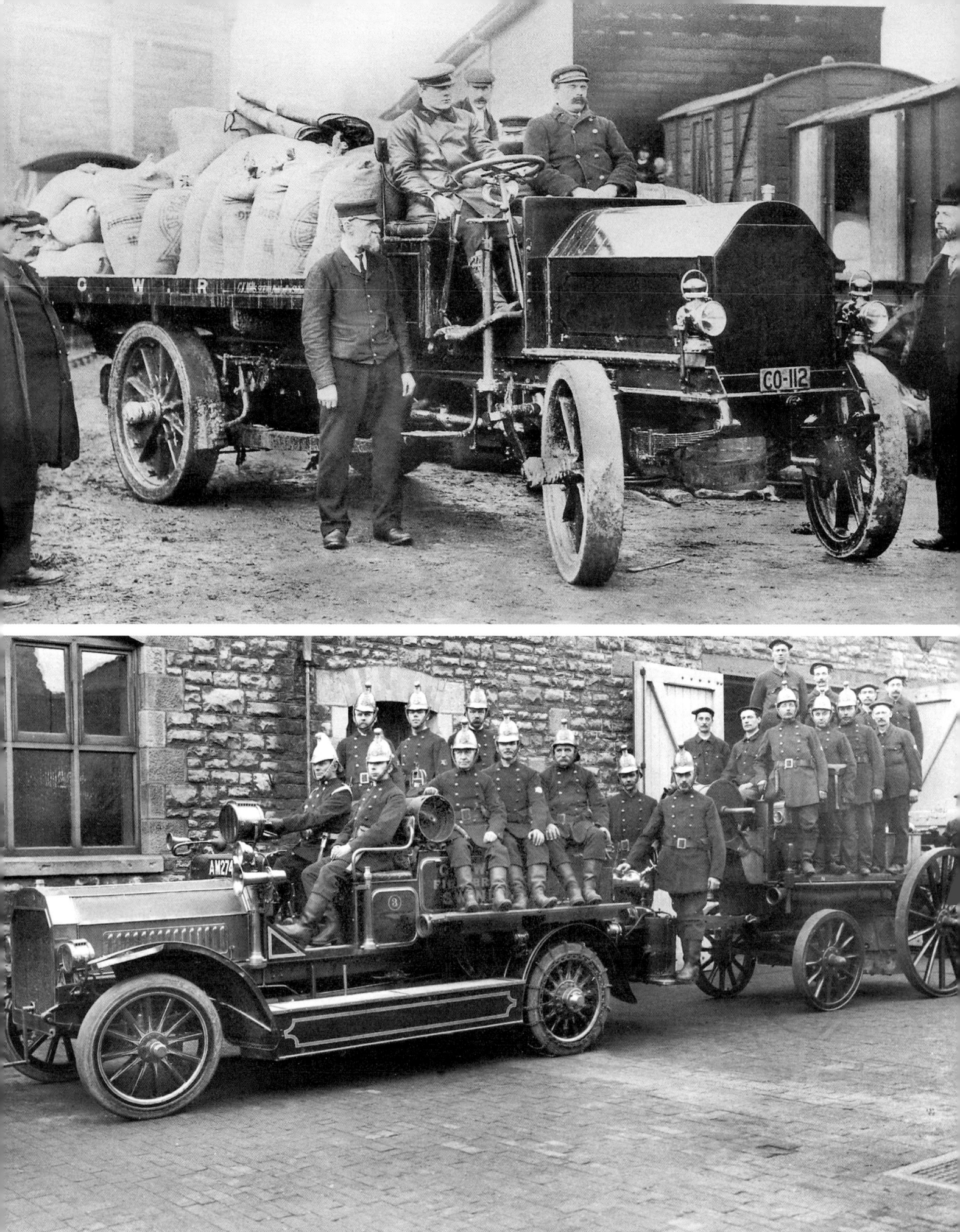

Above **STRAKER SQUIRE PARCELS VAN**
At the start of the First World War, 100,000 men employed by the railways in Britain enlisted in the armed forces. Women quickly filled this void and were used in diverse areas of the industry. The lady pictured has joined the GWR road vehicle department and is assisted by a young lad just visible at the rear. The express parcels service van is a Straker Squire vehicle.

Opposite above **MILNES DAIMLER LORRY**
Whilst a number of the Milnes Daimler chassis was equipped with 20 horsepower engines, some came with 30 horsepower units. This flatbed lorry was so equipped when new in 1905 and is seen with a load at Plymouth around that time.

Opposite below **DENNIS FIRE ENGINE**
Dennis Brothers built bicycles before turning to the automobile business in the early 20th century. The company specialised in lorry construction before the First World War, as the brothers felt this area was an emerging market. Following the conflict, there was a surplus of vehicles used by the armed forces so the focus switched to buses, fire engines and dustbin lorries. This Swindon Works fire engine predates the First World War by two years and was in use to 1956. Coupled at the rear is an oil-fired steam engine which was used previously. The duo is seen in 1916 with the volunteer fire brigade. The fire engine has been preserved.

Above **TRACTOR AND TIPPER TRAILER**
The GWR considered the effectiveness of the road vehicles and took into account the possibility of having a lorry out of action waiting to be unloaded as being wasteful. For trailers and ex-horse-drawn carts, the company thought mechanical horses and tractors allowed greater flexibility and a number were placed in service over the years. A tractor is connected to a tipper trailer above.

Opposite below **SCAMMELL TEN-TON LORRY**
This 10-ton Scammell lorry was purchased in 1929 with at least one other vehicle of the design. Unlike some other tractor-trailer units, the rear was fixed in place.

Below **KNOX TRAILER LORRY**
Purchased in 1918 from the Knox Automobile Company, Springfield, MA, this tractor was paired with a GWR-built two-wheel semi-trailer.

Above **AEC LORRY**
This AEC 3½ ton chassis began life fitted with a charabanc body but was rebuilt in the late 1920s to carry a flatbed. The lorry has agricultural machinery loaded for a show in 1930.

Above **FORDSON TRACTOR AND CONTAINER**

Henry Ford came from a family with a farming background. Following his increasing success with automobiles, Ford turned his attention to achieving similar feats with agricultural equipment. Building several prototypes in the early 20th century, production models began to appear during the First World War and soon became recognised under the brand Fordson. Initially made in the USA, the tractors were later built in Ireland and England. A Fordson tractor is ready with a trailer to receive a BX-type container c. 1930.

Opposite above **KARRIER TRACTORS**

Scammell is perhaps the most well-known producer of mechanical horses, yet Karrier pre-dates the aforementioned design by a few years. Established in 1908 at Huddersfield, Karrier produced a mechanical horse and trailer for the town's Corporation in 1929 known as the Colt. The London Midland & Scottish Railway became aware of the idea and developed the tractor into the Cob which found success. In the late 1930s, the GWR has received a batch of 15 Karrier Cobs, all of which are consecutively numbered and registered in this image.

Opposite below **THORNYCROFT NIPPY LORRY**

Introduced in the late 1930s, Thornycroft's Nippy chassis had a limit of 3 tons and had a speed limit of 30 mph. The body design was left to the discretion of the customer and in this instance, no. A2773 has been fitted with a van body, likely at Swindon.

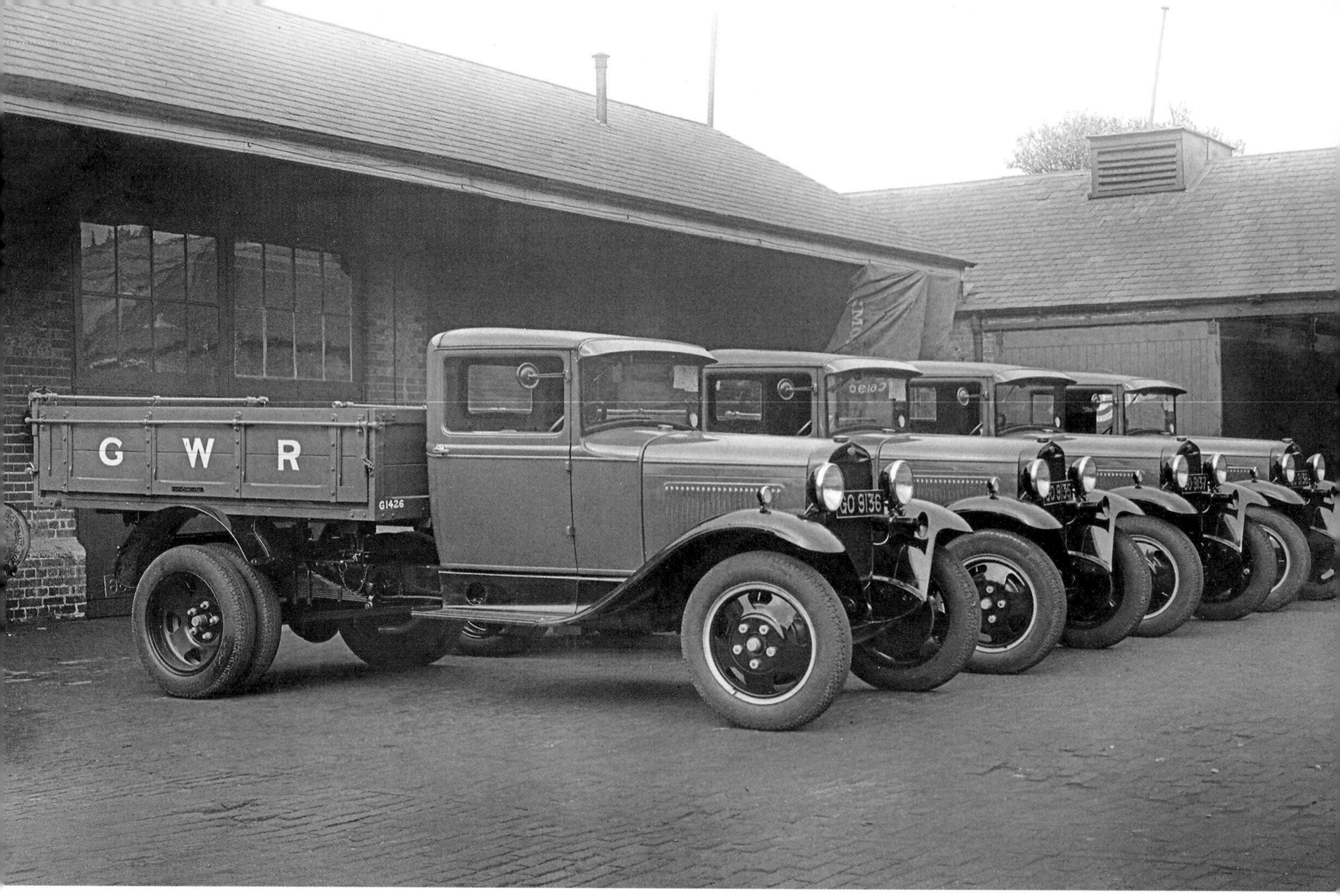
G W R
G1426
GO 9136

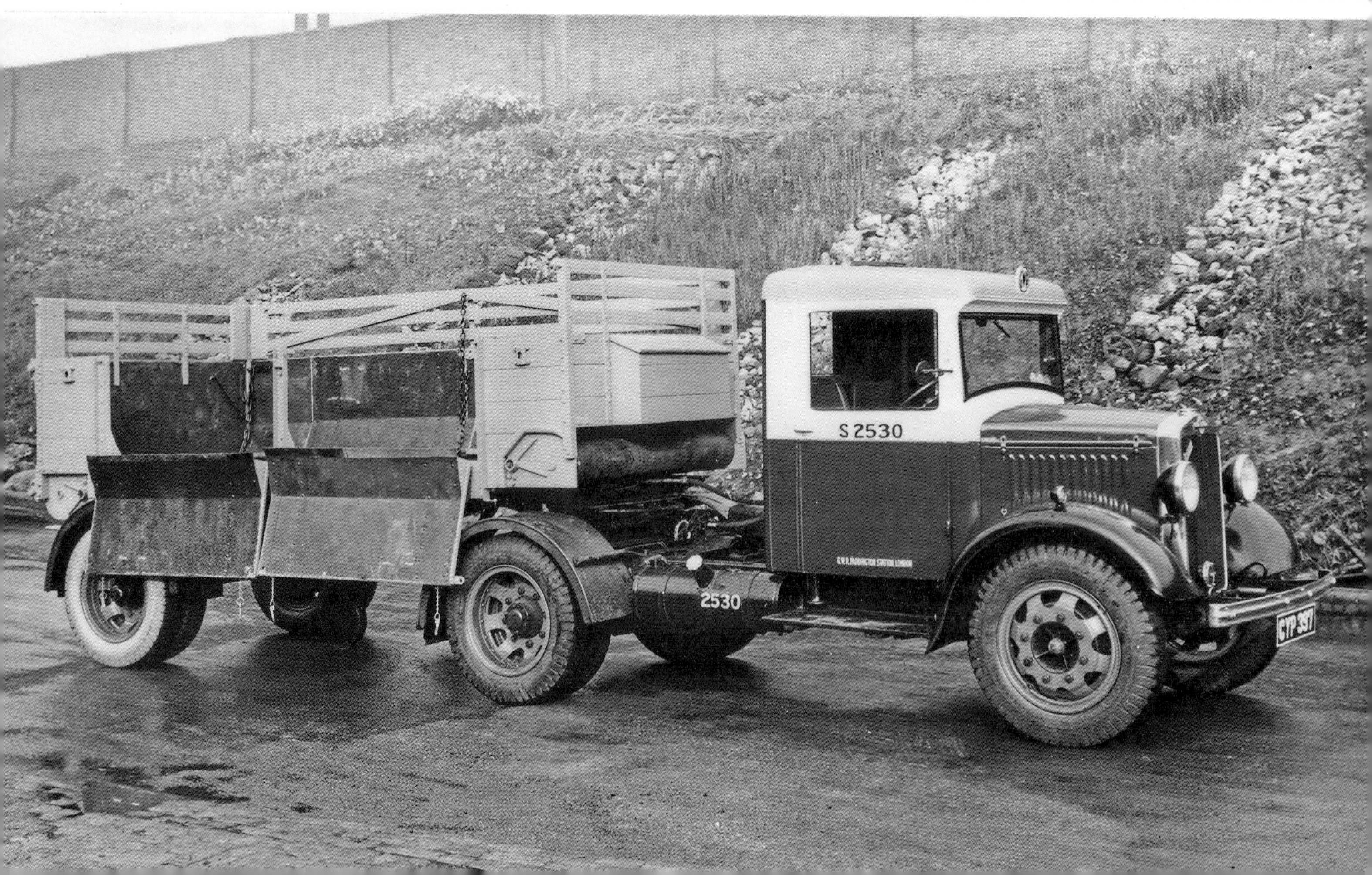
S 2530
2530
CYP 397

Above **THORNYCROFT LORRY**
A 2-ton Thornycroft lorry with flatbed and removable sides is loaded with maize at Lechlade-on-Thames station, north of Swindon, during the mid-1930s. From the late 1920s, the GWR arranged daily or set-time deliveries with local firms from the railhead.

Opposite above **FORDSON TIPPER TRUCK**
A quartet of Fordson BB model 2-ton tipper trucks are seen in the early 1930s. The bed was hydraulically operated to discharge the contents. The Fordson brand covered commercial vehicles as well as agricultural machinery.

Opposite below **MORRIS TRACTOR**
This 6-ton Morris tractor has been paired with an innovative trailer which featured a moveable floor. The feature allowed the load to be removed quickly and was developed by the Principality Wagon Co. Ltd, Cardiff.

Above **CONTAINER AND TRAILER**
The London Midland & Scottish Railway pioneered the use of containers in the mid-1920s. This was done to reduce handling during the shipping process. The London & North Eastern Railway followed suit before the end of the decade, whilst the GWR built containers from 1930. Several sizes existed and some were dedicated to special traffic. The development of the container also necessitated special wagons, as well as trailers for their movement. In this image from the mid-1930s a BK-type container branded for furniture removal sits atop a Dyak G trailer which would have been hauled by a 6-ton Scammell Mechanical Horse. This illustrates the point of the tractor being able to depart whilst the work was carried out increasing productivity.

Opposite above **RANSOMES, SIMS & JEFFERIES ELECTRIC LORRY**
Starting as a manufacturer of agricultural equipment, Ransomes, Sims & Jefferies branched into vehicle construction in the early 20th century. These were initially Orwell model electric lorries of various capacities. The lorries pictured are the 2½-ton version and are at Swindon Works for the fitting of bodies to carry parcels. They went into service during early 1919 and had a top speed of 14 mph with regenerative braking a feature to help recharge the batteries. The Orwell went on to be successful for local authority refuse collection.

Opposite below **HORSE AND WAGON**
Though both petrol and electric lorries were introduced in the early 20th century, the GWR continued to rely on horse power for many years subsequently. At the end of the first decade of the new century, some 3,000 horses were employed by the company and just after Grouping this number had not diminished by a significant amount. In the mid-1930s, nearly half of the horses had retired and for Nationalisation the number was dropping below 1,000. The last horse left employment at Paddington in 1954. A pair of horses is seen here with delivery wagon no. 535 during mid-1937.

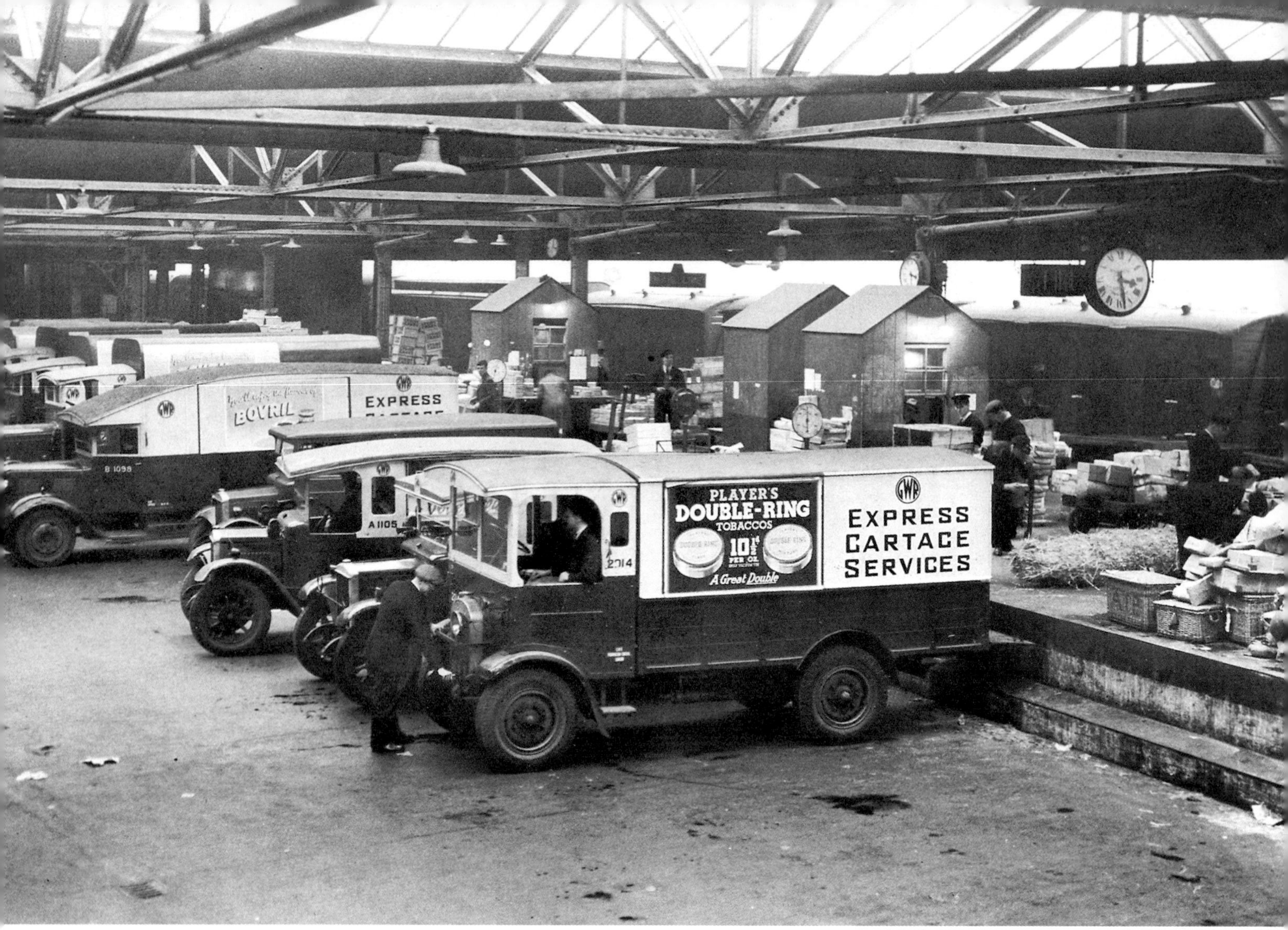
BOVRIL
EXPRESS
B 1098
A 1105
GWR
PLAYER'S
DOUBLE-RING
TOBACCOS
A Great Double
2014
GWR
EXPRESS
CARTAGE
SERVICES

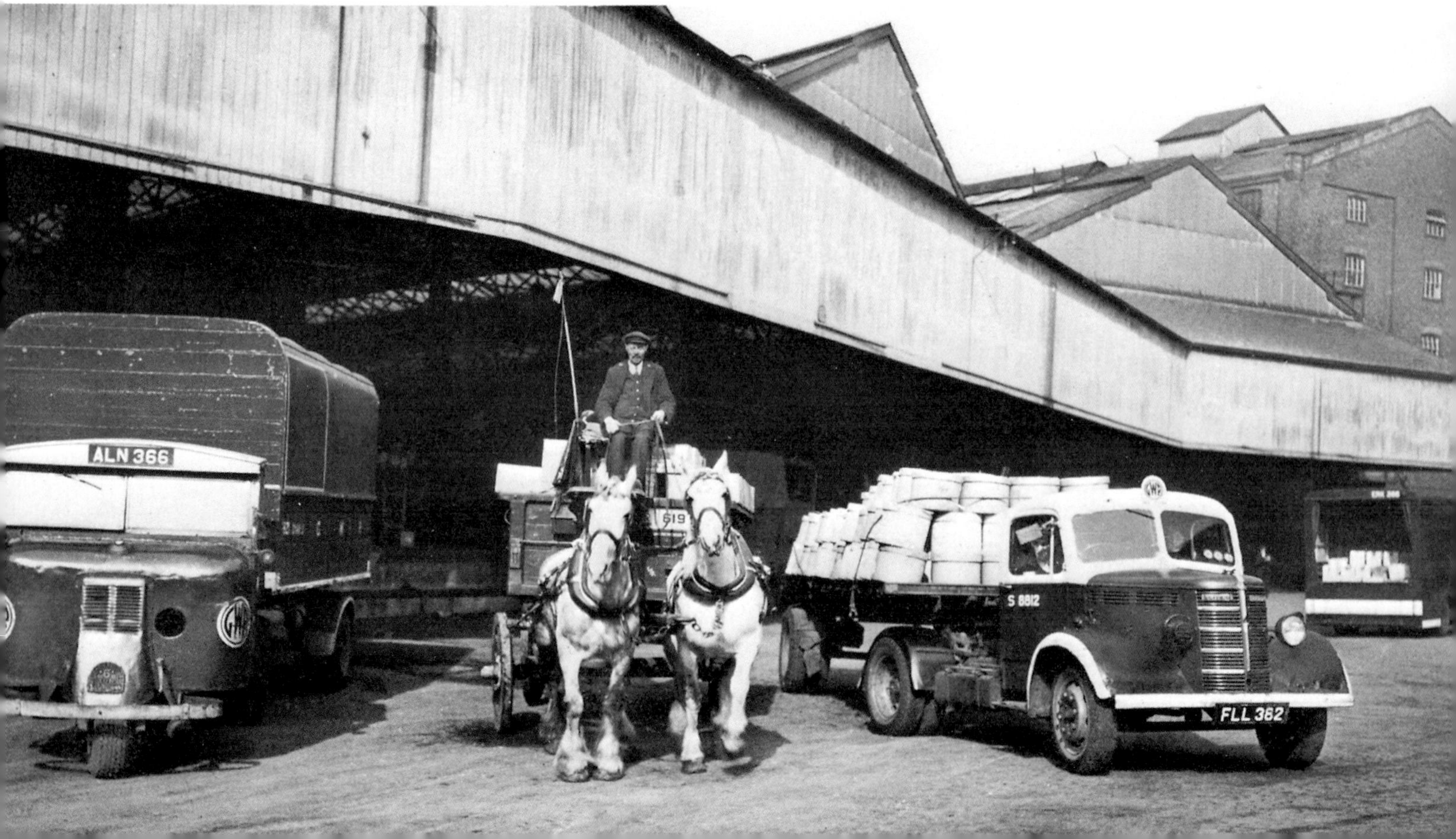
ALN 366
619
S 8812
FLL 362

Above **MORRIS AMBULANCE**
The outbreak of the Second World War saw many changes become necessary. Some of the GWR's life-expired road vehicles were kept in service, such as a Morris van, which was repurposed as a fire engine. In the above instance, a Morris 2-ton lorry has been transformed into an ambulance for use in the Paddington area early in the conflict. Detail alterations include obscuring the headlight for blackout conditions and lining the edges in white.

Opposite above **PADDINGTON GOODS STATION**
Located a short distance to the north west of Paddington station, the goods station was remodelled during the late 1920s. In the mid-1930s, 260,300,000 tons of merchandise were handled there, with 14 platforms 600 ft long provided. A group of lorries are being loaded there in the late 1930s and these include a Thornycroft, Morris Commercials, Comer, AEC and Associated Daimler. Paddington Goods was in use to the 1980s and the site has been cleared and redeveloped.

Opposite below **PADDINGTON GOODS STATION**
A Scammell 3-ton tractor and trailer is on the left, a Bedford tractor and trailer to the right and in the centre is a wagon headed by two horses outside Paddington Goods station in the early 1940s.

STATIONS

Above **ASHTON STATION**
The Teign Valley Railway left the Moretonhampstead & South Devon Railway at Heathfield and reached Ashton in 1882. Later in 1903, the Exeter, Teign Valley & Chagford Railway connected with the TVR at Christow, leaving the main line near Exeter. A sparse passenger service operated along the route, whilst a quarry was also served. The route lasted to 1958 for passengers and 1961 for freight. Ashton station is seen just before Grouping.

Opposite above **SWINDON WORKS ROAD WAGON SHOP**
On the east side of the line from Swindon to Gloucester the wagon department of Swindon Works established their shops. Designated no. 17, the road wagon shop was based on site for the construction and repair of the GWR's road fleet. In the early 20th century around 4,000 were in use and required replacement wheels at a rate of approx. 300 per week. As mentioned, when the motorised road vehicles were introduced, the chassis was generally purchased from the trade and the bodies were made at Swindon according to the GWR's requirements. Some appear to be under preparation or repair here, including bus bodies.

Opposite below **ALFRED ROAD MOTOR VEHICLE GARAGE**
As the number of motor vehicles increased during the 1920s, the GWR required new facilities catering for the stabling and repair of them. A large garage was built at Slough in the mid-1920s, as was a similar facility at Alfred Road, Westbourne Park in the capital, whilst a church was converted in Cardiff. Some of the machine tools used at Alfred Road depot are shown here in the early 1930s.

Above **AUDLEM STATION**
The Nantwich & Market Drayton Railway connected the two towns in 1863. One of the original stations was Audlem around halfway between the two. The route was GWR-operated from the outset and was absorbed before the end of the 19th century.

Opposite above **BAMPTON STATION**
The Exe Valley Railway appeared in the early 1880s to join the Taunton to Barnstable line with the Bristol and Exeter route. Bampton was the first station from the junction with the first mentioned and welcomed services on opening of the first section of line ending at Tiverton during August 1884. The remaining part of the EVR was completed in the following year and the whole railway remained in use to October 1963. Bampton station was later cleared.

Opposite below **BASINGSTOKE STATION**
The short distance between Reading and Basingstoke was connected by a railway built by the GWR in the late 1840s. This was done to the Broad Gauge which prohibited a connection with the London & South Western Railway and a separate station was operated. In the mid-1850s, the GWR was ordered to lay Standard Gauge and mixed gauges were used for a time. Basingstoke station survived to the early 1930s when closed and services moved to the then Southern Railway's station.

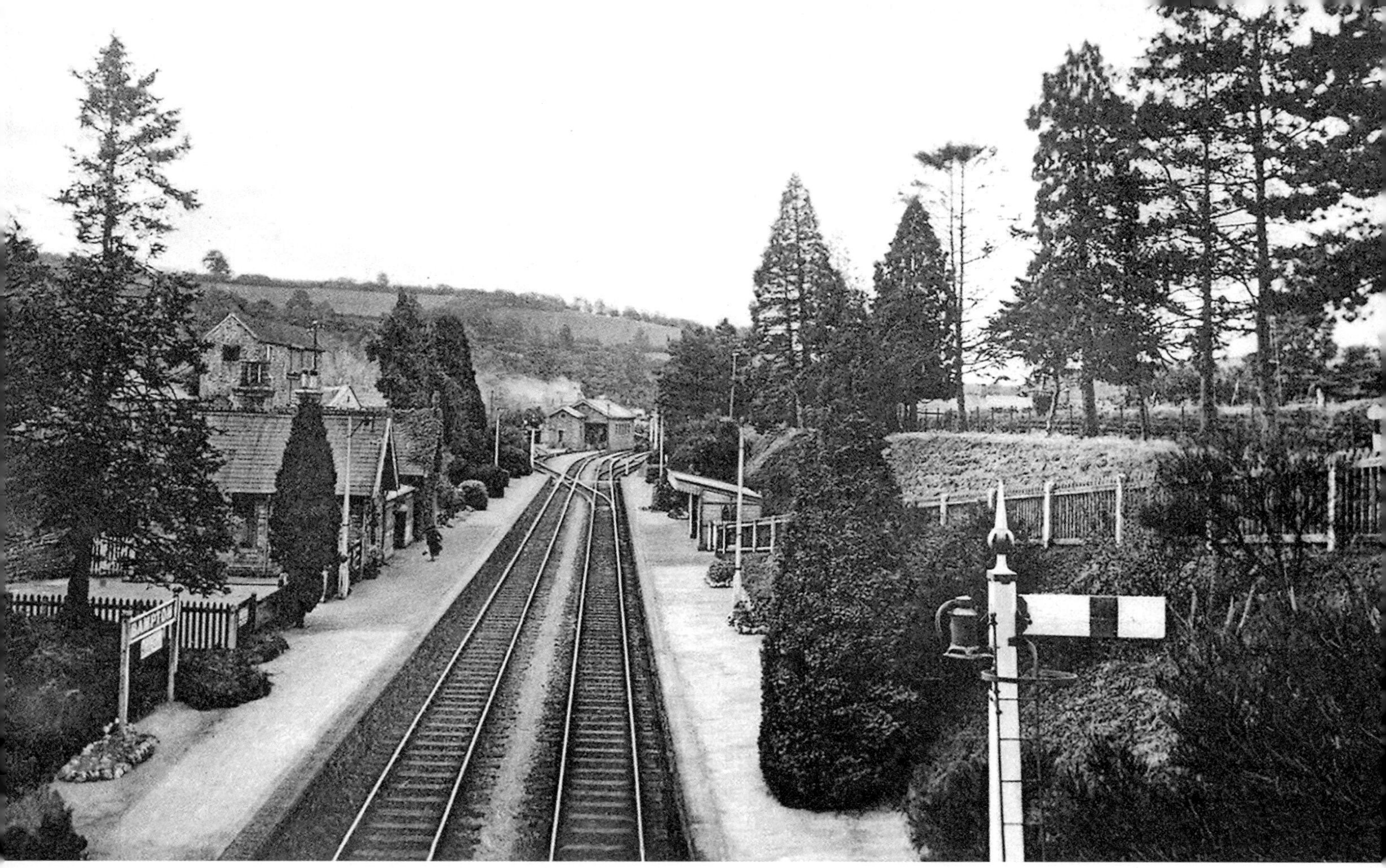

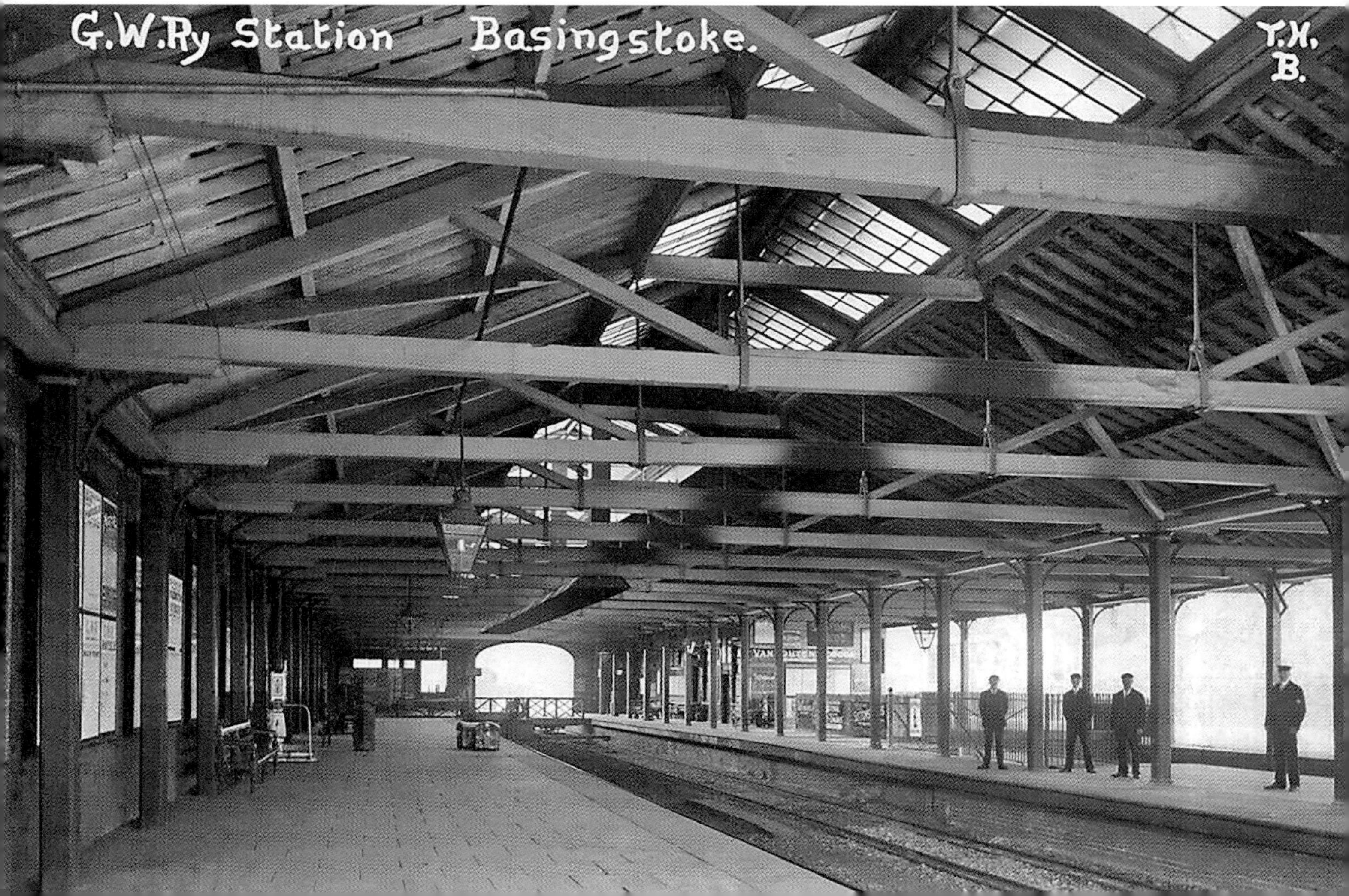
G.W.Ry Station Basingstoke.
T.H.
B.

BRITON FERRY STATION

The South Wales Railway opened a station at Briton Ferry in September 1850. This was in use until 1935 when resited. From July 1924 the station was renamed Briton Ferry West and the nearby Rhondda & Swansea Bay Railway facility was Briton Ferry East until the new station opened. Closed in November 1964, Briton Ferry was provided with a new facility on 1st June 1994.

Above CAMERTON STATION

Exploitation of the Somerset coal field reached a peak in the late 19th century. A branch from the Bristol to Frome line was built to serve a colliery at Camerton in 1882. A station was built which featured a running line, through line and coal siding. The latter is occupied in this image from the early 20th century. Passenger services ceased in the First World War and briefly restored at Grouping but were withdrawn again in 1925. Goods traffic ended in 1951.

Below BOURTON-ON-THE-WATER STATION

A branch from the Oxford, Worcester & Wolverhampton Railway reached Bourton-on-the-Water in early 1862. A connection to Chipping Norton also existed near the main line junction and became the start of a through line between Banbury and Cheltenham which was completed in 1887. Two trains are at Bourton-on-the-Water station here c. 1900.

Above **COOMBE JUNCTION HALT**
The Liskeard & Looe Railway opened in 1862 as a freight enterprise connecting Looe with the Liskeard & Caradon Railway at Moorswater near Liskeard. Passenger services were not offered until 1879 and the mineral traffic began to decline towards the end of the 19th century. Interestingly, the route did not have a connection to the Cornwall Railway, later GWR, and this became a priority. Owing to the terrain, the new line branched to Liskeard in a tight curve. Before the junction opened in 1901, a station was provided for the village of Coombe during 1896 and this later became the point of the junction. The line between Looe and Liskeard continues to operate and, despite low passenger numbers, Coombe Junction Halt is still active.

Opposite above **CHRISTOW STATION**
A view of Christow station on the Teign Valley line from the early 20th century. Opened on the Exeter, Teign Valley & Chagford Railway in 1903, the station was in use to June 1958.

Opposite below **DIDCOT**
Though the GWR reached Didcot in 1840, the station was not established until 1844 when a branch to Oxford opened. At this time a shed was built on the junction and saw an enlargement carried out in the late 1850s. A coal stage was built, later upgraded to a ramped stage with water tank during the 1900s. A full-scale rebuild of the shed was carried out in the early 1930s, though the coal stage remained in use. Following closure in 1965, the depot became the Didcot Railway Centre which continues to operate on the site.

Above NEWBURY STATION

The Berks & Hants Railway between Reading and Hungerford was favoured over a London & South Western Railway scheme from Basingstoke to Swindon via Newbury. Opened during December 1847, the B&HR was later extended to Devizes in 1862. Newbury station was built with the first section and later became a junction for the Didcot, Newbury & Southampton Railway. This opened between Didcot and Newbury in 1881 and a decade elapsed before the line reached Southampton. The company was taken over by the GWR at Grouping. Before the end of the 19th century, Newbury became the connecting point for a branch to Lambourn. Newbury station continues to serve passengers, though the other connections have been removed.

Opposite above LELANT STATION

The last new Broad Gauge line to be built was the St Ives branch, completed in June 1877. One of two intermediate stations opened with the route was Lelant, located to the north of St Erth where a junction was made with the West Cornwall Railway. A Standard Gauge line was added in 1888 before full conversion in 1892. The station at Lelant continues to serve locals and holidaymakers.

Opposite below LOSTWITHIEL STATION

Lostwithiel station opened with the Cornwall Railway in May 1859 as part of the first phase of construction from Plymouth to Truro. The second section arrived in Falmouth four years later. In the late 1860s, Lostwithiel became the departure point for the Fowey branch, yet a more convenient connection was created from Par in 1874 and the original line was mothballed in 1880. Before the end of the century this was reopened and continues to be active, though passenger services have been withdrawn.

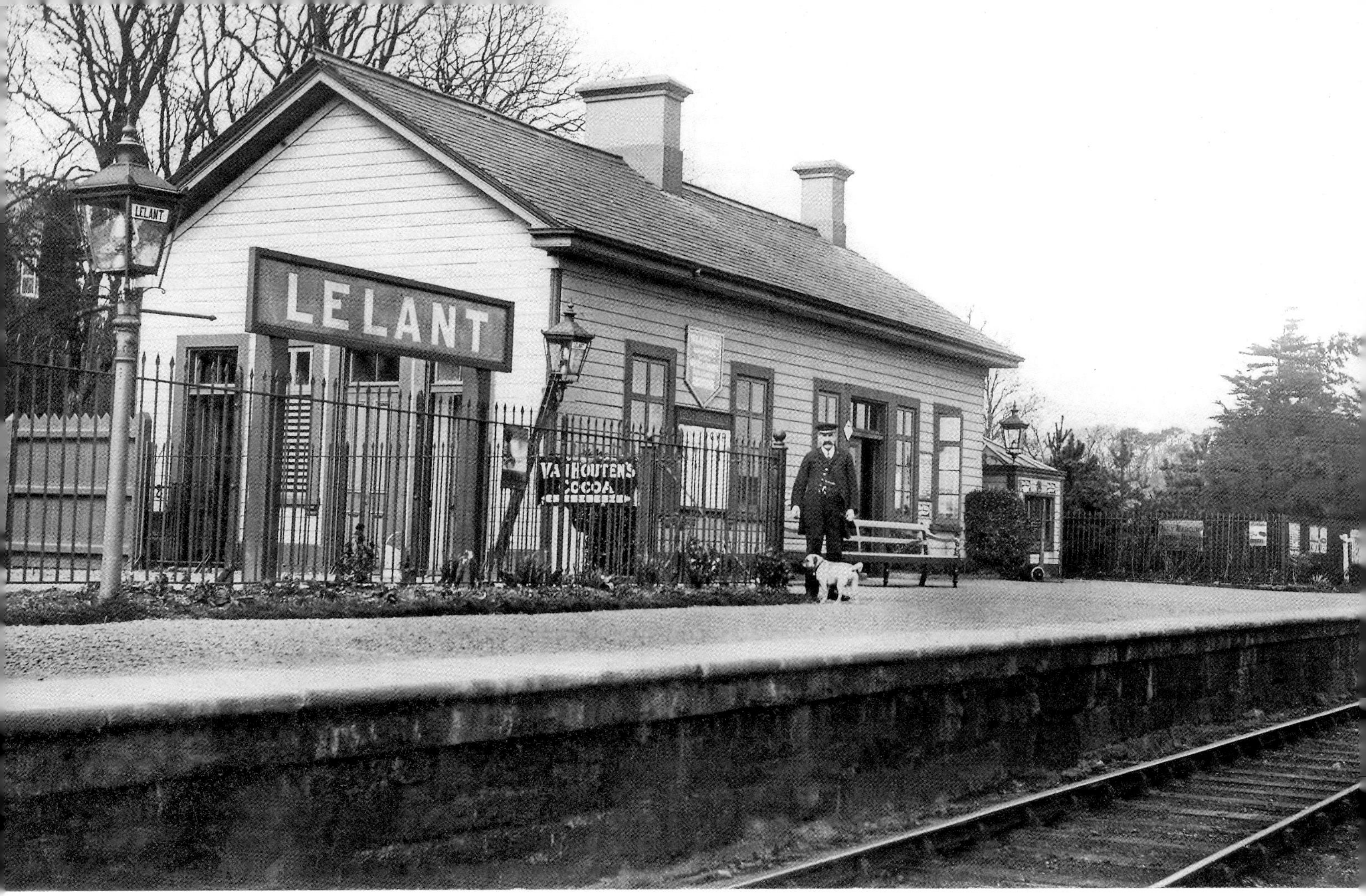
LELANT
LELANT
COCOA

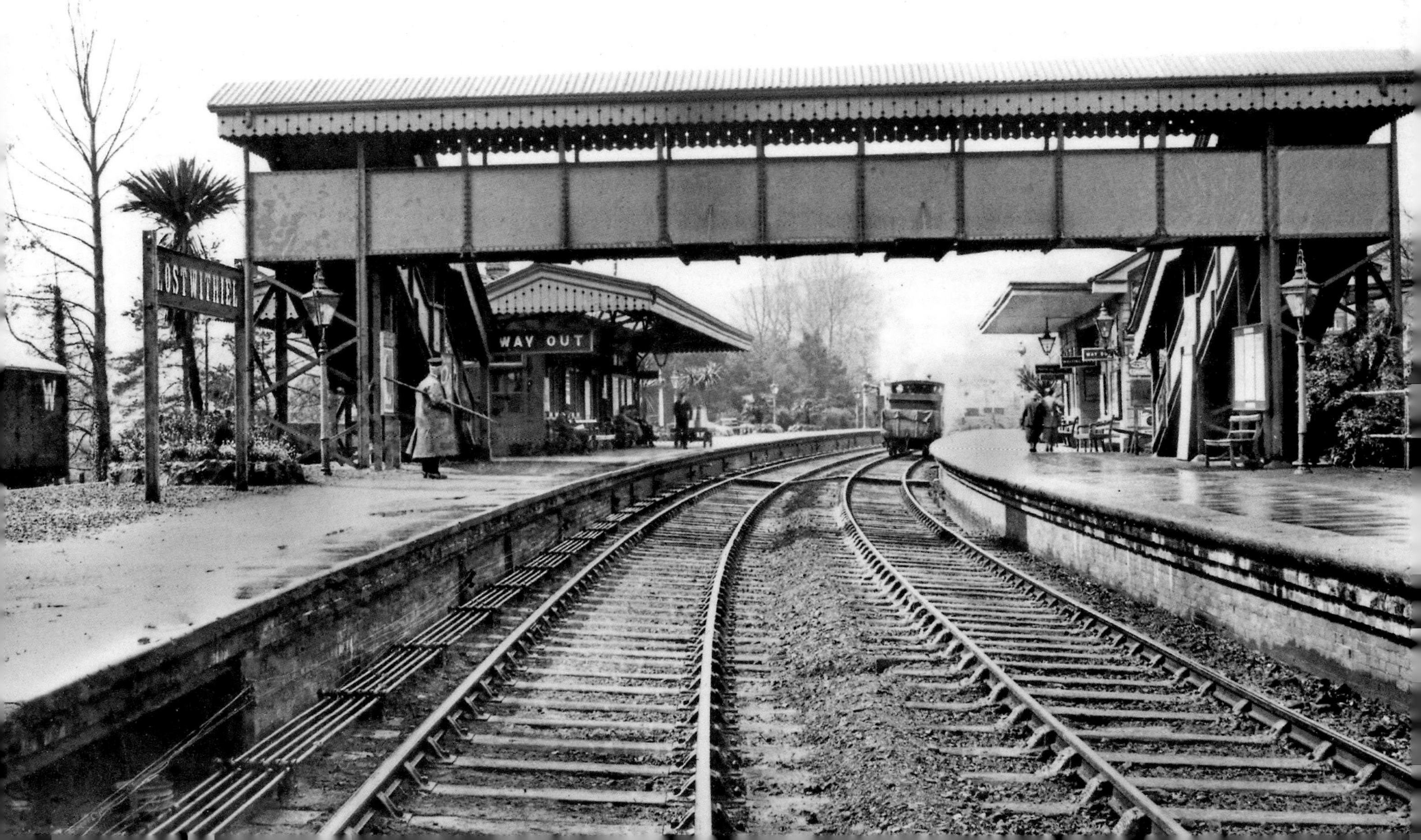
LOSTWITHIEL
WAY OUT

Above **PADDINGTON STATION**
A motor tricycle was introduced in 1910 for use on deliveries in the London area. One is seen with driver at Paddington station.

Below **LUSTLEIGH STATION**
A branch to Moretonhampstead was completed in July 1866 and the last stop before the terminus was Lustleigh station. A train is seen approaching, c. 1900.

Above **PEMBROKE DOCK STATION**

The exterior of Pembroke Dock station is pictured in the early 20th century. This was the terminus of the line from Whitland and opened in 1864, though the route was not fully complete until 1866. Built to Standard Gauge, access to the main line was not possible until 1868.

Below **PENGAM & FLEUR-DE-LIS STATION**

From 1st February 1909 to 1st July 1924, Pengam & Fleur-de-Lis station used this title, starting as Pengam in mid-June 1865 when opened. Briefly known as Fleur-de-Lis station, the facility changed back to Pengam (Mon) in 1926 which was in use to closure at the end of 1962.

Above **PENRHIWCEIBER STATION**
Penrhiwceiber station closed in 1964, yet was later resurrected in 1988. This overview of the station dates from the early 20th century before renamed Penrhiwceiber Low Level station after Grouping.

Below **PWLLHELI STATION**
The line was originally to continue beyond Pwllheli but the plan was abandoned. This left the station badly sited and a new facility had to be opened in 1909. The station has been recorded shortly after that date.

Above **PEWSEY STATION**
Pewsey station opened on the Berks & Hants Extension Railway in 1862 and continues to serve the local village.

Below **RODWELL STATION**
The GWR and L&SWR made a joint effort to connect the Isle of Portland with Weymouth. This line opened in 1865, with Rodwell station a later addition in 1870. Passengers and staff pose for the camera, c. 1900.

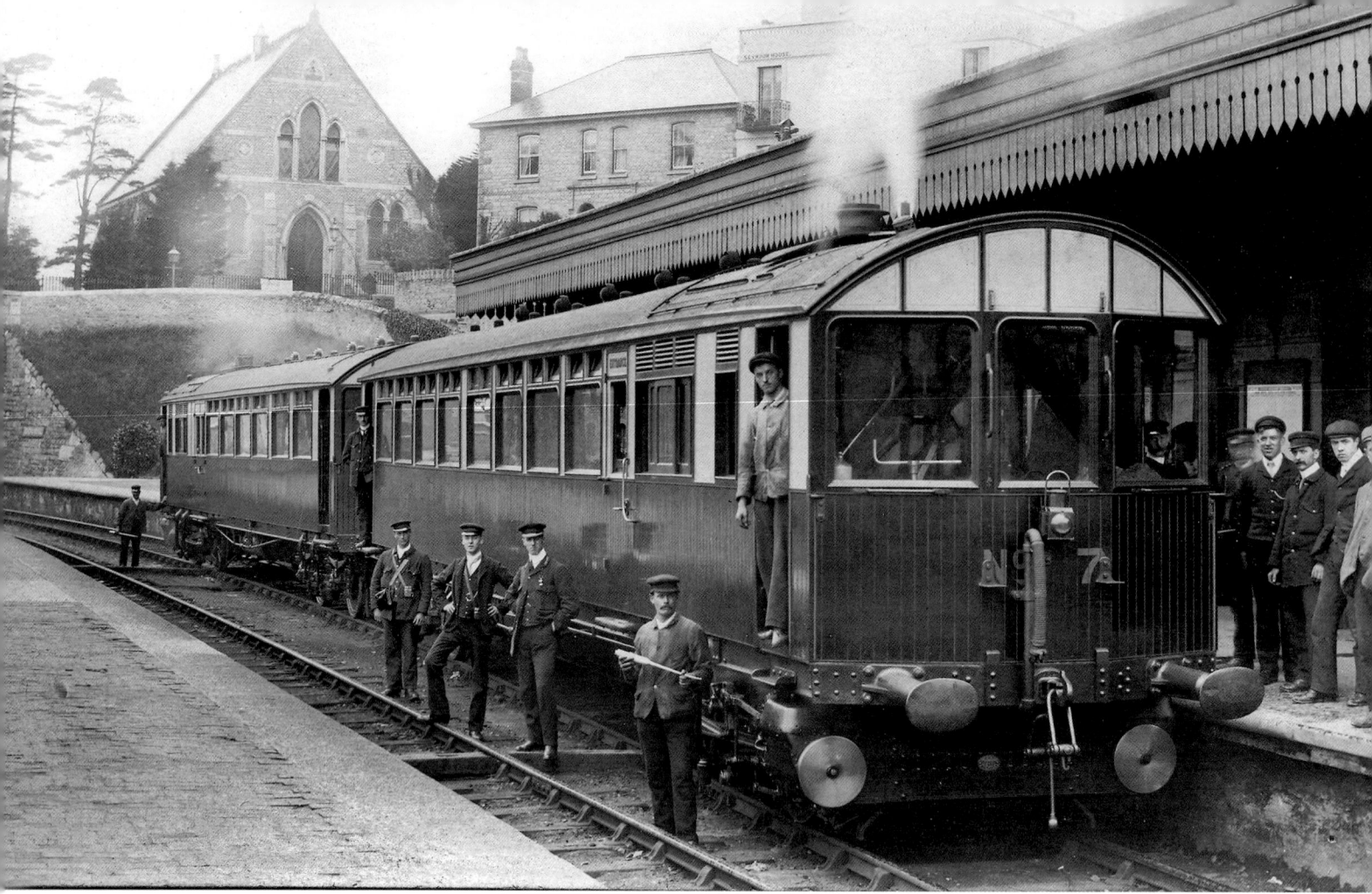

Above **SALTASH STATION**
On the west side of the Royal Albert Bridge, Saltash station was in use by May 1859 and operated by the Cornwall Railway. In the early 20th century, steam rail motor no. 7 and a second unit are seen at Saltash. No. 7 was new in 1904 and had seating for 54 passengers.

Opposite above **SOUTHALL STATION**
Following the opening of the GWR main line in 1838, a station for Southall was added in 1839. To the east of the station, a branch to Brentford Dock started services during 1859. Recently the station has been completely rebuilt as part of the Crossrail project. In the background are two local landmarks: Southall Water Tower, now apartments; Southall Gas Holder. Allegedly, the water tower was castellated at the request of Queen Victoria who had to pass the structure on the way to Windsor.

Opposite below **ST CLEARS STATION**
The South Wales Railway connected the principal places in the area over a period of time in the 1850s before being taken over by the GWR. St Clears station was on the section from Carmarthen and Haverfordwest opened in January 1854. The station went on to serve the town to 1964 and there have been unsuccessful attempts to establish a new facility. A train of clerestory carriages and one of cattle wagons is seen at St Clears in the early 20th century.

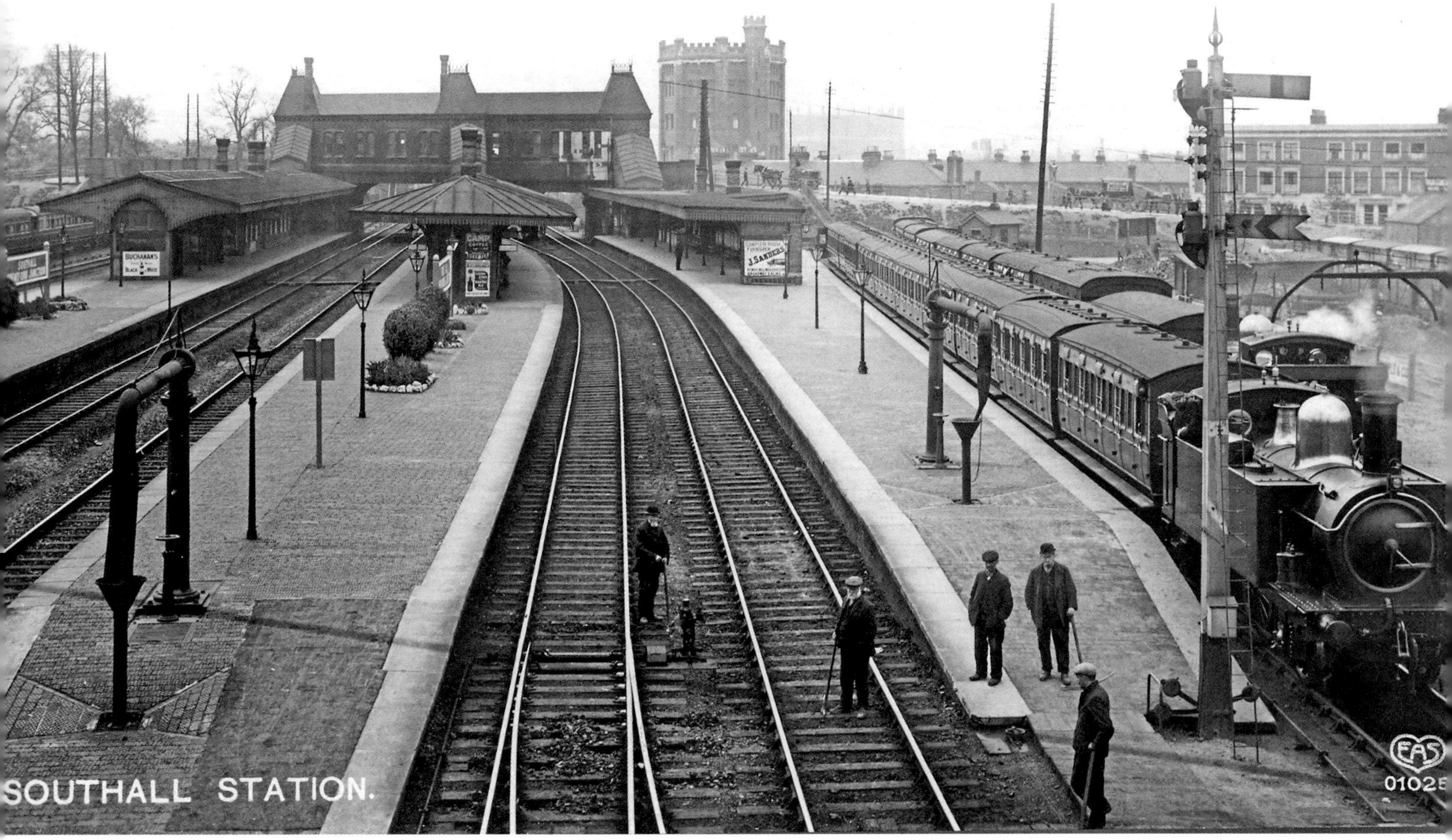
SOUTHALL STATION.
BUCHANAN'S
BLACK & WHITE
J. SANDERS
EAS
01025

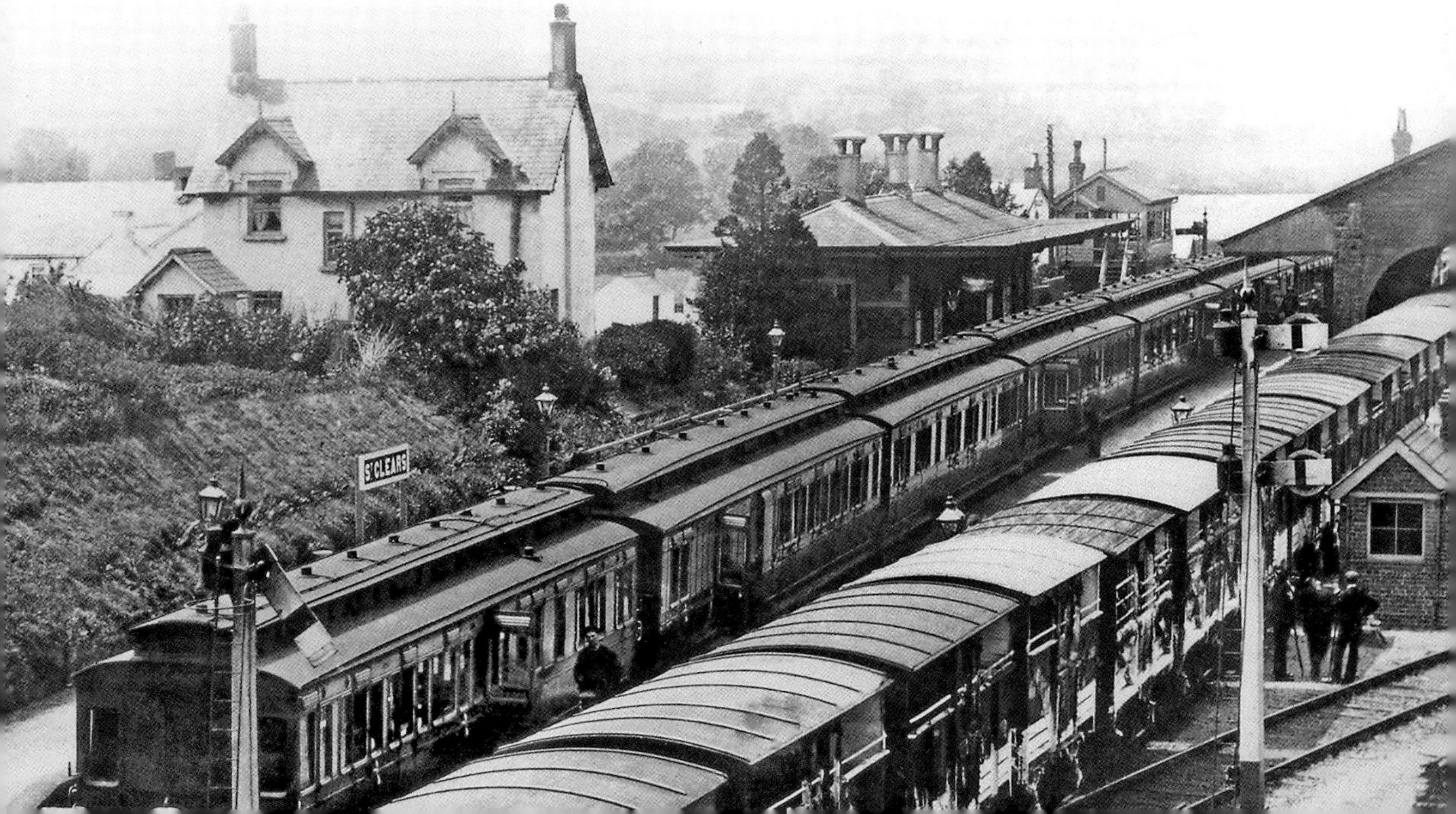
ST CLEARS

Above **STAPLETON ROAD JUNCTION STATION**
The Bristol & South Wales Union Railway's route from Bristol to New Passage for crossing the Bristol Channel was originally planned in the 1840s, but was not realised until early 1864. On the English side of the railway, Stapleton Road station opened in September 1863 with five others. Just over a decade later, the GWR and Midland Railway built a line to Clifton which also connected with the docks at Avonmouth. Stapleton Road Junction then developed as a busy station with four platforms. The change in traffic has subsequently reduced the facility to just two platforms and the buildings have been demolished.

Opposite above **THEALE STATION**
The Berks & Hants Railway opened Theale station, to the west of Reading, in late 1847. The station is still active though the footbridge has been rebuilt and the buildings cleared. This scene was captured from Station Road looking east around the time of Grouping.

Opposite below **TINTERN STATION**
The Wye Valley Railway was promoted to connect Monmouth with the South Wales Railway at Chepstow. Authorised in 1866, a financial crisis disrupted funding and the scheme did not resume until 1874 and completed on 28th October 1876. Tintern was an original station but passed a short distance to the east of the village. As a result, landowners and businesses petitioned for a private branch to run into Tintern. From the outset, the GWR operated the line and later absorbed the WVR in the early 20th century. Relying on tourist traffic, by the 1950s this had switched to the roads causing the end of passenger services in 1959. Freight lasted another five years, though a quarry at Tintern continued to be connected to Chepstow until 1990.

Above WATCHET STATION

The West Somerset Railway was promoted in the 1850s to run from Norton Fitzwarren to Watchet where there was a harbour. The line was completed in late March 1862. Watchet station was a terminus for 11 years when the Minehead Railway extended westward. Both undertakings were operated by the Bristol & Exeter Railway and the company was absorbed by the GWR in 1876. The MR was also taken over in the late 19th century whilst the WSR lasted to Grouping. Freight traffic was withdrawn in the mid-1960s, whilst passenger trains ceased in 1971. From 1976 the route was gradually reopened by the West Somerset Railway heritage trust.

Opposite above WILMCOTE STATION

The area around Stratford-upon-Avon saw a number of railway schemes reach completion in the 1850s. The Birmingham & Oxford Junction Railway was a major project for the GWR and passed by Stratford-upon-Avon to the east. The Stratford-upon-Avon Railway built a branch in 1860 from the B&OJR at Hatton, with Wilmcote station opened at this time. In the early 20th century, Wilmcote was rebuilt and continues to serve the village.

Opposite below YELVERTON STATION

The South Devon & Tavistock Railway was laid from Plymouth in 1859 and saw an extension to Launceston completed in the mid-1860s. Yelverton station was a later addition to the route, opening during 1885 to provide a junction for the Princetown branch. This latter survived to 1956 and Yelverton closed with the line to Tavistock at the end of 1962.

BIBLIOGRAPHY

Allen, Cecil J. *Titled Trains of Great Britain*. 1983.

Barrie, D.S.M. *A Regional History of the Railways of Great Britain: Volume 12: South Wales*. 1994.

Baughan, Peter E. *A Regional History of the Railways of Great Britain: Volume 11: North and Mid-Wales*. 1991.

Cattell, John and Keith Falconer. *Swindon: The Legacy of a Railway Town*. 1995.

Cook, Kenneth J. *Swindon Steam 1921-1951*. 1974.

Griffiths, Roger and Paul Smith. *The Directory of British Engine Sheds and Principal Locomotive Servicing Points: 1 Southern England, the Midlands, East Anglia and Wales*. 1999.

Kelley, Philip J. *Great Western Road Vehicles Appendix*. 1982.

Kelley, Philip J. *Road Vehicles of the Great Western Railway*. 1973.

Quick, Michael. *Railway Passenger Stations in Great Britain: A Chronology*. 2009.

RCTS. *Locomotives of the Great Western Railway: Parts One to Twelve*. 1951-1974.

Rogers, Colonel H.C.B. *G.J. Churchward: A Locomotive Biography*. 1975.

Russell, J.H. *A Pictorial Record of Great Western Coaches Including the Brown Vehicles Part I (1838-1913)*. 1972.

Russell, J.H. *A Pictorial Record of Great Western Coaches Including the Brown Vehicles Part II (1903-1948)*. 1973.

Semmens, Peter. *History of the Great Western Railway: 1. Consolidation 1923-29*. 1985.

Semmens, Peter. *History of the Great Western Railway: 2. The Thirties 1930-39*. 1985.

Semmens, Peter. *History of the Great Western Railway: 3. Wartime and the Final Years 1939-1948*. 1985.

Thomas, David St John. *A Regional History of the Railways of Great Britain: Volume 1: The West Country*. 1973.

Also available from Great Northern

Gresley's A3s

Peppercorn's Pacifics

British Railways Standard Pacifics

Gresley's V2s

Gresley's D49s

Gresley's A4s

Gresley's B17s

Thompson's B1s

Stanier's Jubilees

The Glorious Years of the LNER

The Glorious Years of the GNR

The Glorious Years of the LMS

John Ryan's Express